ANSWERING GOD'S CALL TO QUIET

*Finding Strength and Peace
for a Pressured Life*

Nonfiction Books by Neva Coyle

Abiding Study Guide
Answering God's Call to Quiet
Daily Thoughts on Living Free
Diligence Study Guide
Discipline tape album (4 cassettes)
Free to Be Thin, The All-New (with Marie Chapian)
Free to Be Thin Lifestyle Plan, The All-New
Free to Be Thin Cookbook
Free to Be Thin Daily Planner
Free to Dream
Freedom Study Guide
Learning to Know God
Living by Chance or by Choice
Living Free
Living Free Seminar Study Guide
Making Sense of Pain and Struggle
Meeting the Challenges of Change
A New Heart . . . A New Start
Obedience Study Guide
Overcoming the Dieting Dilemma
Perseverance Study Guide
Restoration Study Guide
Slimming Down and Growing Up (with Marie Chapian)
There's More to Being Thin Than Being Thin (with Marie
    Chapian)

A Devotional Daybook
by Neva Coyle

ANSWERING GOD'S CALL TO QUIET

Finding Strength and Peace for a Pressured Life

BETHANY HOUSE PUBLISHERS

MINNEAPOLIS, MINNESOTA 55438

Published by Bethany House Publishers
A Ministry of Bethany Fellowship, Inc.
11300 Hampshire Avenue South
Minneapolis, Minnesota 55438

Printed in the United States of America.

Library of Congress Cataloging-in-Publication Data

Coyle, Neva, 1943–
    Answering God's call to quiet : finding strength and peace for a pressured life / by Neva Coyle.
      p.   cm. — (A devotional daybook)
    ISBN 1–55661–938–3 (pbk.)
    1. Spiritual life—Christianity. 2. Spiritual exercises. 3. Quietude.
4. Peace—Religious aspects—Christianity. 5. Stress (Psychology)—Religious aspects—Christianity. 6. Time management—Religious aspects—Christianity. I. Title. II. Series: Coyle, Neva, 1943–   Devotional daybook.
BV4501.2.C685   1997
248.4—dc21   97–4735
                                                      CIP

NEVA COYLE is a bestselling author whose ministry is enhanced by her gifted motivational speaking and teaching. She is presently a prayer ministry director in her church and is president of Neva Coyle Ministries. She is also the founder of Overeaters Victorious. Neva and her husband make their home in California.

Requests for materials or speaking information should go to:

Neva Coyle
P.O. Box 1638
Oakhurst, CA 93644

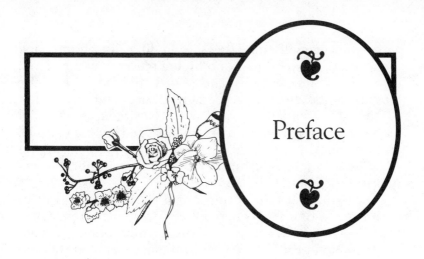

Preface

I STOOD IN RESPONSE to the worship leader's invitation. *Come into the Holy of Holies . . .* we sang.

"Shut up!" the mother beside me whispered between clenched teeth. "You are driving me crazy!" Her second grader responded with a pout.

Enter by the blood of the Lamb . . . the music continued.

"Got a mint?" the man in front of me asked his wife. She began rummaging through her purse.

Come into His presence with singing . . .

"Take her to the nursery," the young father sitting behind me commanded his wife.

"I can't," she said curtly. "She's got a runny nose. They won't let her in."

"Oh, great," he snapped.

Oh, brother, I said to myself. *Just what I didn't need this morning.* With a busy, stress-filled week behind me and yet another stretching out in front, I had looked forward to this morning's worship service. I needed the quiet, the opportunity to step away from my everyday life, to focus on God and draw strength for the days ahead. Shutting my eyes, I tried to distance myself from the surrounding distractions and concentrate on worship. Soon I felt a presence at my elbow.

"Excuse me, Neva," the man whispered, "but the kitchen is locked, the snack lady is late, and some idiot locked all the partitions in the boys' bathroom. And . . ." I didn't wait for him to finish before I grabbed my purse, Bible, and notebook and headed out to solve the problems. After all, it was my job. Worship would have to wait until my responsibilities were handled—again.

Such interruptions during worship happen to all of us from time to time, but when you're part of a church staff it can happen weekly. It goes with the territory when you work and worship in the same place. I no longer serve in that position, but if I'm not careful, it can still happen: my worship experiences, whether at church or at home, can be sabotaged by distraction. Moments with my Master contaminated with the noisy stuff of ordinary life. Even in quiet worship times alone, I can find myself fighting interruptions from phones, family, and friends. What's worse, my own mind can become a battleground of *inner* distractions: rambling thoughts, worries over money, concerns about how I'm going to get everything done that day, or just meaningless chatter. All tugging at me to get my focus off God and onto the mundane aspects of everyday life. And it doesn't happen only to me. How about you? Do the noise and distractions of everyday life rob you of inner peace and quiet? Does your devotional life suffer because, with all of life's distractions, you find you just can't keep your mind on God?

Do you ever wish for a few moments of complete silence—a buffer between you and the everyday noisy world? Modern life has so many competing sounds, it's no wonder human beings are driven to distraction. Our work environments, polluted with the sounds of whining copy machines and the jack-hammer staccato of computer printers, are also filled with prerecorded music piped into our workspaces to distract us from all the other sounds. Even if our office is at home, phones jangle our nerves and fax machines scream their high-pitched signals when connecting.

Our homes, ordinarily thought of as our haven from the noisy world, are also filled with the sounds of growling dishwashers, grinding disposals, and groaning washing machines. Hair dryers, electric razors, and pulsating showerheads shatter our morning peace. And who hasn't had their only free weekend in a month invaded by the noises of the neighbors' lawnmowers, weed-eaters, and blaring boomboxes?

Any one sound alone would not be that big a deal, but when you consider the constant bombardment of noise we all put up with every day, it *does* affect us. Too much sound, say the experts, affects not only our work, but also our tranquillity. Researchers frantically search for innovative ways to either deaden sound or eliminate it altogether.

For Christians, it's more than just our auditory environment that is being invaded. Our spiritual environment is being polluted by the sin-filled sounds of our civilization as well. Voices of compromise and immorality hammer relentlessly at our spiritual sensitivities. Hurtful memories leave us callused and unable to hear the Holy Spirit's low whispers of quietness and comfort. Temptations scream at us through both audiovisuals and the print media, and decadence boldly displays itself even in the supermarket checkout line.

Little by little, this bombarding of our senses has become so familiar we no longer notice we are being manipulated. Yes, it's true, day in and day out through radio and television we are assaulted by media sound bytes designed to control our behavior and shape our opinions. And yet we allow it to continue, even in our homes. We simply don't think about what it's doing to us, and ironically we often find comfort in the steady noise.

For many, silence has become so uncomfortable it is avoided altogether. We arrive home from our noisy work environments and immediately invite Peter Jennings to update us on the most recent world events. Or we let CNN deliver the bad news of the entire world every twenty-two minutes. We even let talk shows degrade our sensibilities by parading in our own living rooms things that should never be talked about in public. And our children, so used to the noise of our modern existence, find it difficult to live with one moment of silence—preferring to do their homework with the crashing and screaming of their favorite alternative-style band mainlined into their brains via headphones.

9

Have we all gotten so used to the worldly, even evil, distractions surrounding us that we have crossed some invisible point of no return? Is there no chance of developing sharp spiritual listening skills and fine-tuning our hearts to hear the whispered voice of God? Must He, too, shout for our attention?

In many churches these days, worship services often leave little or no room for silent meditation, or time for seeking inner quiet. Worshipers are kept busy, even entertained, the services carefully orchestrated to allow no "awkward" silences.

Cornelius Plantinga commented on this modern trend in a *Christianity Today* article, published July 17, 1995: "Even contemporary worship, in some church settings, fills in silences with an emcee's patter or with snappy Christian music from which all the rests have been removed." And whatever quietness our fast-paced worship doesn't snatch from us, our demanding church calendar does. It's not unusual for something worthwhile, and deserving of our support and attendance, to fill every free night of the week. Church can become such a whirlwind of activity that time for solitude and silence are nonexistent—even foreign and strange. For many Christians, personal quiet time is compromised or doesn't exist at all. Sadly, it is often replaced by "doing God's work."

Most of us know the wonderful experience of going to a retreat, far away from our daily routine. Excited for this rare opportunity to get away and enjoy the quiet, usually in a beautiful setting, we pack our suitcases and tuck in our Bibles and notebooks—plus a few other books or magazines, just in case the silence proves unbearable. Once there, we are startled to rediscover the soft sounds of breezes rustling through trees, of croaking frogs and singing crickets. We find in our silence that brooks still babble, and that screen doors still squeak. And, most of all, we are thrilled to discover that God still whispers and our hearts still yearn to speak softly in response. How many of us, at the end of such a weekend, take a deep breath and promise ourselves to do this more often? Yet, despite our resolve to approach life more quietly, do we then plunge back into the speeding merry-go-round of activity we call normal, productive life? Any thought of

...ng a daily practice of quietly enjoying God's pres-
...ets buried under the noise of life once again.

In this DEVOTIONAL DAYBOOK, I invite you to explore
with me the concept of waiting quietly, silently, before God.
The idea is simple: *stilling the inner noise of our minds as we
withdraw periodically from the outer noise of our regular, normal
life.* But it's not as easy as it sounds. Even though it is a viable
and valuable form of personal, ongoing devotional worship,
it can be a challenge. Yet I believe that the devotional life
of even the busiest Christian can, and in fact *should*, include
silence as much as Bible reading, praise, and petition.

Through the following thirty devotional readings and response pages, I offer you the opportunity to answer God's call
to quiet—to shut out the disturbing noises of your life and
discover anew, or for the first time, the spiritual value of bal-
ancing your life with moments of stillness and silence in His
presence.

Come and rediscover quiet. I promise you practical instruction and creative ideas on how to find the time and
place to be silent, how to begin to include silence in your
daily routine, and how to expand your capacity for silence.
And finally, how to extend the fruit of peace and calmness
found through devotional silence into the whole of life.

What I offer in the pages of this book is not to be con-
fused with what the world offers. I'm not promoting meditation for meditation's sake. Nor am I suggesting anything
beyond biblically sound devotional practices. This book is
not about attaining inner peace through New Age tech-
niques of guided imagery or visualization.

My purpose is to entice you to reestablish *God's* peace,
calm, and quiet assurance deep within your soul. To discover
an oasis of fresh water for your parched spirit in the middle
of a dry, noisy world. But I must warn you: don't be surprised
if, in the end, you thirst for more—much more—peace, stillness, and silence once you have answered God's call to quiet.

11

Contents

How to Use This Book

THIS DEVOTIONAL STUDY is designed to fit easily into a busy schedule. It is divided into six sections, with five chapters in each section. By reading a chapter each day, you can complete the study in just thirty days. Take a few minutes each day to read the suggested Scripture. Apply the Scripture selection to your life by answering the questions at the end of each chapter. Writing your own response in the space after questions will help you better establish the scriptural truths in your life.

If the book is used in a group study, members can study the five chapters of a section during the week and then meet as a group to discuss the material. In this way the book will take six weeks to complete, or longer, depending on the needs of the group. The study is easily adaptable to an established women's ministry group or a Sunday school class.

For groups using the study, suggested leader's guidelines and discussion questions are included at the end of the book.

"Come with me by yourselves to a quiet place and get some rest."

MARK 6:31

Section I

Come Away

"COME AWAY," JESUS SAYS. "Come with me." An invitation. A call. Yes, right in the middle of our busy, responsibility-packed lives, Jesus speaks to us with as much reality as when He spoke those words to His first disciples. An invitation, a call we either answer or ignore. But can we get away? How will we find a way to respond? Pressed on every side with responsibilities and worthwhile projects, how can we get even a moment *away* without guilt and the risk of getting behind on our fully-packed schedules?

No one could ever be busier than Jesus was. His ordinary days were filled with curious crowds pressing Him with their needs, plying Him with their questions, and pressuring Him for more. He came, after all, to dwell among the people. His life was people, and His heart was touched by their needs. Even then, some days were more pressing than others. Mark 6:31–32 tells it like this: "Then, because so many people were coming and going that they did not even have a chance to eat, he said to them, 'Come with me by yourselves to a quiet place and get some rest.' So they went away by themselves in a boat to a solitary place."

On hearing the news that John the Baptist had been cruelly assassinated by Herod, Jesus wanted solitude. Just a little while away from his pressure-filled schedule to mourn His terrible loss. But it wasn't so easy to get away, even for a moment of private grief. The crowd followed, once again proving themselves needy, and this time, hungry as well. Jesus responded to their need, miraculously feeding the five thousand that followed Him to this secluded spot, then finally called it a day, once again seeking solitude.

As much as He loved the people, He needed more—He

18

needed to be alone. And so do you and I.

With our own busy lives, sometimes filled to the brim with purpose and the needs of those we love, we often find it difficult, self-centered, or nearly unthinkable to satisfy our own need for quiet. Just a few moments away from it all to pray, to think, to refresh ourselves and gather strength for life's next "go-around" can seem indulgent and selfish.

Yet Jesus often went to the mountains or the beach to be alone. What's more, He recognized the need for His disciples to get away from the demands of the crowd as well. And so it is with us. This book is your invitation to answer His call— to spend some precious time alone with Him.

"Come away," He invites. "Come with me."

For a few moments, forget your responsibilities and think of yourself as a little girl once again, holding a bright bouquet of spring flowers for the King. You bow low in His presence. "Majesty," you whisper as you extend the colorful blooms toward His outstretched hand.

"My daughter," the King whispers as He accepts your gift. "Come with me," He repeats softly. "Take my hand and come. . . ."

What will you do? Will you go with Him? Can you see yourself accepting His invitation and going to a place where you can be alone with Him?

Chapter · 1 ·

Come With Me . . .

Read Matthew 14.
Reflect on these words from Mark 6:31–32:

> *Then, because so many people were coming and going that they did not even have a chance to eat, he said to them, "Come with me by yourselves to a quiet place and get some rest." So they went away by themselves in a boat to a solitary place.*

What does Jesus mean by this invitation to "Come with me . . ."? It's not always possible to get away for more than just a few minutes or even short distances. Even so, it is imperative to get away. To spend time in His presence, experiencing Him.

For example, when the house is quiet, while everyone else is still sleeping, is a perfect time to accept the Lord's invitation. Maybe you can't leave the house, but you can go to another, quieter room and spend that very special few quiet minutes in the presence of the Lord and Savior who beckons, "Come with me."

Susanna Wesley, the godly mother of evangelists John and Charles Wesley, had seventeen children. By anybody's standards, that was a busy household! The story is told that when she sat in the kitchen with her apron pulled up over her head, her children virtually tiptoed around her. Each and every one knew that this was Susanna's time with her Lord and Savior. Her time for quiet reverie with God.

Like the example of Susanna, you, too, can leave your responsibilities for a little while. For a few moments, separate yourself from those things that demand your attention. My own mother would once in a while look at the stacked dinner dishes at the end of an exhausting day and sigh, "Oh well, they'll still be there in the morning." Can we accept the fact that our responsibilities will be right there waiting for us the moment we return from our quiet moments of devotion and prayer?

And, while you're at it, leave your concerns behind as well. Give yourself permission to go unhindered, putting space between yourself and your life—to be with Jesus himself.

Can you manage to draw away from someone needing you, wanting you, or demanding your attention—for a few minutes—to be apart with Christ? Try letting yourself do nothing but bask in the presence of God.

Think of yourself as invited by the Lord to be alone with Him. Can you picture the Lord with His hand outstretched? "Come . . ." He invites. What would you like to say to Him once you are away from all the others? Picture yourself in a boat riding across the gently rippling water. Life is happening on the shore behind, and awaits on the shore ahead. But for now, relax; you are coming away at *His* invitation. Away from pressures and responsibilities to enjoy each other's company. For this majestic moment, all else is held in suspension. You are responding to Him. A moment in the presence of His Majesty. I wouldn't miss it for the world, would you?

Do whatever it takes to answer His call to quiet. Give up your coffee break at work, turn off the TV, or put down the paper. Go for a long walk alone at lunch. This is a wonderful opportunity to spend a few moments with Him. Bow low and respond, "Yes, Majesty." Take His hand and "get in the boat."

Consider these words of wisdom:

Quiet times, devotions, or whatever we may call our

practice, is a *place* and *space* we choose to create in our lives so that we can meet with God. In this age of driven and busy people, it is a frequently neglected discipline. But without a devotional practice, daily life becomes shallow and vague. With a vital devotional time, all of our lives are opened to the privilege and pleasure of God's presence.

—Stephen D. Frye,
Quiet Time Dynamics

Enjoy these words of beauty:

O Thou, in whose presence my soul takes delight,
On whom in affliction I call,
My comfort by day and my song in the night,
My hope, my salvation, my all!

Dear Shepherd! I hear and will follow Thy call;
I know the sweet sound of Thy voice;
Restore and defend me, for Thou art my all,
And in Thee I will ever rejoice.

—Joseph Swain

———————

What has interfered or prevented you from coming away with the Lord for quiet times in the past?

What would you have to do to momentarily lay aside the distractions of an ordinary day?

23

Would you feel guilty for doing so?

Today's responsibilities:

My scheduled events include:

Some of my pressing concerns are:

Further thoughts I have or distractions I need to deal with in order to create *place* and *space* for my quiet times:

Possible places I can go to be "away" include:

Best time to "come away" would be:

Write a new or renewed commitment to keep a regular quiet time here:

Chapter · 2 ·

...From the Familiar

Read Mark 8:22–26.
Reflect on these words from verse 23:

He took the blind man by the hand and led him outside the village. . . .

Considering how difficult it is for some of us blessed with good sight to make changes, I can't help but pause, realizing how difficult it must be for a blind person to be led away from all he knows to be familiar. Yet, in order to experience Jesus at this most personal level, isn't it what He does for all of us?

Certainly that's what He did for the disciples. Can you imagine living with the miraculous day after day? Wouldn't so many miracles put them in danger of considering them nothing more than business as usual? How long before the majestic acts of Jesus would be seen as merely *ho-hum, another healing* or *oh well, another evil spirit cast out?* Familiarity can be a dangerous, blinding trap—not only for the disciples of history but also for you and me, believers today.

When I first moved to the mountains, each trip into town through the rugged countryside was an adventure. I marveled at the snow-covered peaks of the distant high Sierras. I slowed my car to take in the wonder of a brilliant rainbow stretched across a valley below. Billowy clouds hugging the nearby hilltops seemed so picturesque, and the winding roads held promise of still another scenic view at every turn. But that was six years ago. It's different now. I'm familiar with it all. I drive the nine miles into town rehearsing my grocery list or making a mental map of errand-determined destinations. I check my watch to see if I have time to stop at the gas station or drugstore before church. It's not unusual to get so lost in my own thoughts that the magic of some of the most beautiful scenery in all of California's historical gold rush country goes completely unnoticed. What once inspired wonder has now become habit. Habit has replaced seeing. The scenic highway has become simply the shortest route between two points, home and town. And what's more, I thought it would never happen.

The same thing can happen in our relationship with Christ. Our prayer life can become simply the shortest route between our need and His provision. The miracles He does for us every day can become almost matter-of-fact. Sadly, the wonder of His grace can be received more out of habit than heart. Our devotional life can change from exploration and excitement to little more than dedicated duty. We can become so familiar with our routine, we lose sight of *Him*. And we thought it could never happen. At least I didn't—until recently.

Not long ago I sensed the Lord urging me to do something different in my quiet times. To put aside all prepared Bible study books or devotional materials and pick up an old hymnal I had bought at a yard sale. "I'm not sure," my inner self whined in protest. "I'm so used to doing it this way." Finally I gave in and rediscovered a rich "family" heritage I had ignored far too long.

Then one day I felt an inner tugging at my heart concerning my elaborate prayer lists and organized method of making sure all my prayer concerns were covered. *Ouch!* If I didn't lift these needs to the Lord, what would I do in my prayer time? I am, after all, somewhat of an intercessor. What do intercessors do if they aren't busy with the business of petitioning? This method is so *familiar*. In a way, I had become as blind as the man in Mark 8:23. And it can happen to anybody—even you.

Thankfully, when that happens we can depend on Jesus

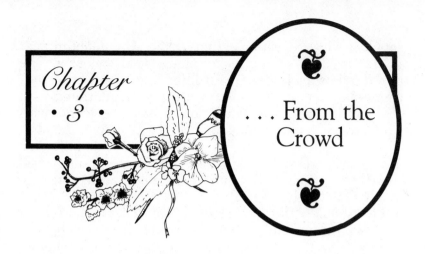

Chapter
· 3 ·

... From the Crowd

Read Mark 7:31–37.
Reflect on these words from verse 33:

He took him aside, away from the crowd. . . .

Ever wonder not only about *what* Jesus did, but why? I do. Consider, for example, the words for today's reflection.

A man is brought to Jesus for healing. His friends have heard that Jesus is in the area, and His healing reputation has preceded Him as usual, so they bring their friend. I would have done it. If I had heard that Jesus was in the neighborhood and my friend needed a touch, I would have joined the escort group without hesitation. After all, such opportunities shouldn't be missed.

However, as thrilled as I would have been that my friend was healed, I probably would have been a little disappointed that Jesus took him away to do it. I'd have wanted to see it happen up close, firsthand.

I can't help but look at this passage and wonder why? Why would Jesus take him aside, away from the crowd, to heal him? Maybe the answer can be found by looking at the crowd—in fact, crowds in general.

Crowds are a mix of many types of people; their motives are varied, and their faith is at different levels. Crowds are an interesting conglomerate of curiosity seekers, honest believers, and haughty skeptics. The nosy stand shoulder to shoulder with the genuinely interested. The doubtful next to the inquisitive. The seeker alongside the mocker. The crowds following Jesus were no different than any other run-of-the-mill crowd. In addition, they were infiltrated with those watching for even the slightest shred of evidence with which to end, or at least discourage, the mission of the Master. The legalists were there, as were Jesus' true followers. The arrogant as well as the desperate. Those who followed the latest spiritual fads beside those truly waiting, praying, and hoping for the Messiah.

We shouldn't forget that what Jesus did, He did for the man, not the audience. He was motivated by the need—not by some carnal, human hunger for reputation or premature glory—but the need of a simple deaf man.

Because His focus was the individual, not the group, Jesus took him aside, away from the crowd. And He does the same today.

I can remember wonderful camp meetings, conferences, and moving worship services in my church. I can mentally list exciting neighborhood Bible study sessions and Sunday school classes. Such experiences of Christian fellowship and worship are important for my growth as a Christian. But many, if not most, of my life-changing, ministry-establishing, need-meeting encounters with Jesus happen when I respond to Him in private—away from the crowd. When I take time to answer God's nudge to step away from the crowd and all it represents, I am called into ministry, filled with love for those who are hurting, forgiven of my sin, filled afresh with the Holy Spirit, and even physically healed. It's when I answer His invitation to come away, to let Him take me aside, that I receive new precious things from Him. New insight into Scripture, new hope and perspective. It's when I let myself be drawn away from the crowd that my heart is stilled in the face of confusing and pressing difficulties. It's when I pull away from common opinion and preferred worship styles to be with my Savior that I find my fears hushed and my faith renewed.

You see, crowds have pretty much remained the same—and the work Jesus wants to do in and through me requires more than public worship and even good Christian fellowship. Jesus wants to meet with me in private—away from prying eyes, curiosity seekers, and especially skeptics. Just Him and me. In privacy, away from the crowd, He opens my ears that have been deaf to His voice. Loosens my tongue to speak words He alone can give.

When I am removed from peer pressure, accepted cultural behaviors, and current religious fancies, He speaks to me through His personal presence. When I step away from the confusion of group expectations, where personal inhibitions stifle my response to Him, He heals the deafness of my soul. He loosens the bonds around my heart and frees me to listen, to learn, and to love Him in ways that are not for public view.

Away from the crowd my relationship with Jesus deepens in intimacy, strengthens in love, and becomes very personal.

And it can happen for you, too. If you make it a regular practice to leave the crowd behind, to meet with Jesus unencumbered by others' expectations, you can have the same intimate closeness with the Lover of your soul. If you will but take the time to go "behind closed doors" with the Master of the Universe, you will discover a very personal relationship with a Savior who longs to be your friend.

Take this unparalleled opportunity that Jesus offers and create a space and place in your life to get away from the crowd, away from their dictates and especially their negative influences. I can't promise you healing, hope, and heartfelt union with Him; that's a promise He himself reserves to make. I can't tell you how much He loves you and how significant you are to His kingdom. Those are things He wants to say to you—not in public, but to you . . . alone, away from the crowd.

Consider these words of wisdom:

> We are often hindered from giving up our treasures to the Lord out of fear for their safety. This is especially true when those treasures are loved relatives and friends. But we need to have no such fears. Our Lord came not to destroy, but to save. Everything is safe that

we commit to Him, and nothing is really safe that is not
so committed.

—A. W. Tozer, The Pursuit of God

Enjoy these words of beauty:

> I come to the garden alone,
> While the dew is still on the roses,
> And the voice I hear, falling on my ear,
> The Son of God discloses.

> He speaks, and the sound of His voice
> Is so sweet the birds hush their singing,
> And the melody that He gave to me,
> Within my heart is ringing.

> And He walks with me, and He talks with me,
> And He tells me I am His own,
> And the joy we share as we tarry there,
> None other has ever known.

—C. Austin Miles

What "people groups" do you belong to that could be defined as a "crowd"?

What influences do you think your "crowd" has on you?
Positive:

Negative:

What emotional price do you think you might have to pay if you were to "step away" a bit to be alone with Christ?

What practical steps could you take to assure yourself the privacy you desire?

Write a new or renewed commitment to "step away from the crowd" below:

Chapter · 4 ·

... From Your Concerns

Read Luke 8:1–15 and 10:38–42.
Reflect on these words from 10:42 and 40:

> *"Mary has chosen what is better. . . ."* But Martha was distracted. . . .

Living in a real world with real demands and pressures, I immediately want to jump to Martha's defense. Of course, I am learning to have more and more "Mary" moments—uninterrupted, uncluttered, and undisturbed joy with Christ. But I have to admit, I've had more "Martha" moments of wanting to be with Jesus, but bogged down with family, schedules, and errands instead.

You know how it goes: breakfast for the family, gathering homework together, packing lunches, getting your poky child to the school bus on time, laundry, grocery shopping, housework, outside job, taking the car to the repair shop— on and on it goes. Legitimate and necessary demands all wrapped up in the care and concern for our families. Let's face it, if Jesus came to my house to eat, I know perfectly well who would do the cooking. After, of course, soccer practice, piano lessons, dropping off the cookies for the women's ministries bake sale, and returning overdue books to the library while I'm out.

Yet all of this constant activity—which we may feel is perfectly legitimate and fulfilling our God-given responsi-

37

bilities—can stand in the way of our receiving from the Lord.

In Luke 8:14, in the parable of the sower, Jesus refers to "those who hear, but as they go on their way. . ." In other words, as they hustle their way through everyday life, just like you and me, "they [the seeds of God's Word] are choked by life's worries."

It reminds me of my Grandmother Sampson and her little patch of green grass so lovingly sown, yet threatened by weeds. Grandma was a determined woman. In a mountainous area of Southern California's Mojave Desert, she determined to grow not only a garden but a small patch of lawn outside her front door. She raked the ground smooth, handpicked it free of rocks, tilled the clay-imbedded dirt, and hauled in rich, sandy topsoil. Then, when the ground was perfect, she sowed her seed. Watering twice, sometimes three times a day, she eventually had grass. However, not only did she have the promise of a little patch of green, but spreading through her precious lawn was devil's-grass—a hybrid form of wild crabgrass. It looked okay to me. "Why not just leave it alone?" I asked childishly.

"Because it will choke out the seeded grass," she answered, "and it will spread into the garden." Then on her hands and knees, pulling furiously at the offending growth, she declared between clenched teeth, "And I won't have it!"

Grandma put up with a lot of inconvenience and difficulty living out there in the desert, but devil's-grass in her lawn pushed her almost beyond her limit.

We too have to deal with the "devil's-grass" in our lives if we want to grow in Christ. Our devil's-grass may be the truly unreasonable and unnecessary burdens we've taken upon ourselves, but it may also disguise itself as legitimate concerns: concerns that threaten to choke out the seeds of truth God desires to plant, tend, and bring to maturity in us. We need to understand that the invitation to spend time before the Lord in prayerful recognition of His presence includes the fact that we will have to step away from even the reasonable and regular demands of our everyday life. To recognize that the "worries of this life" threaten our time in God's presence, and to take Grandma Sampson's determined attitude: "I won't have it!"

38

You see, the worries and busy activities of this life can so dominate us, they can actually make God's word unfruitful and unproductive in our parched hearts and hungry souls. Who says we have to watch the news every night for an hour? Who says we must bake ten dozen cookies for the bake sale? The Lord? Our overdeveloped sense of duty and responsibility? Our personal need to be needed?

Our everyday concerns, the ordinary stuff of life, can demand so much of our attention that we actually forget to turn them over to the Lord. And how can He remind us to do so if we refuse to step even a little distance away so He can speak to us about them?

Jesus understands and addresses such concerns when He says, "Do not worry about your life, what you will eat or drink; or about your body, what you will wear. Is not life more important than food, and the body more important than clothes?" (Matthew 6:25). His words directly release all believers from the bondage of anxiety over basic necessities. How much more, then, should we abandon worry and concern over the nonessentials!

By first stepping away from our concerns for time alone with God, we can concentrate on simply enjoying His presence, and eventually we will be able to completely release our concerns to Him. I'm convinced that only when we orient all of the details of our lives to God will we be able to realize that life's meaning isn't found in the successful management of our daily concerns, but in being willing subjects—obediently, purposely stepping away from those never-ending, demanding details in response to the invitation of our all-wise, all-powerful, all-loving King.

Can you do it? Can you take the time to turn aside from even the legitimate concerns of your life long enough to spend unhurried moments with Jesus—choosing, as Mary did, *what is better?*

———

Consider these words of wisdom:

> Look at the birds of the air; they do not sow or reap
> or store away in barns, and yet your heavenly Father

feeds them. Are you not much more valuable than they? Who of you by worrying can add a single hour to his life? And why do you worry about clothes? See how the lilies of the field grow. They do not labor or spin. Yet I tell you that not even Solomon in all his splendor was dressed like one of these.

—Jesus (Matthew 6:26–28)

Enjoy these words of beauty:

Sitting at the feet of Jesus,
O what words I hear Him say!
Happy place! so near, so precious!
May it find me there each day!
Sitting at the feet of Jesus,
I would look upon the past;
For His love has been so gracious,
It has won my heart at last.

Sitting at the feet of Jesus,
Where can mortal be more blest?
There I lay my sins and sorrows,
And when weary find sweet rest.
Sitting at the feet of Jesus,
There I love to weep and pray,
While I from His fullness gather
Grace and comfort every day.

Bless me, O my Savior, bless me,
As I sit low at Thy feet;
O look down in love upon me,
Let me see Thy face so sweet;
Give me, Lord, the mind of Jesus,
Make me holy as He is;
May I prove I've been with Jesus,
Who is all my righteousness.

—Author Unknown

———

What concerns do you have that feel like "devil's-grass" threatening to choke out the better "planted seed" in you?

How does what you listed keep you from stepping away from your concerns to meet privately with the Lord?

If you really believed the words of Psalm 138:8, how would that change the way you approach a quiet time with God?

If God were really to take care of what concerns you today, how would your attitude toward your day's schedule or current responsibilities change?

Write a prayer relinquishing your concerns to God as you step away from them and into His presence.

Chapter
• 5 •

... From Unbelief

Read Mark 9:14–27.
Reflect on these words from verse 23:

"Everything is possible for him who believes."

Picture this: a young father is walking down the street with his son. The boy has few friends because he has sudden and frightful attacks that are fearful to watch. Without warning, the child can be thrown to the ground, foam at the mouth, and stiffen for several alarming minutes while the attack runs its course. No one can even get the boy's perspective on what happens, for he is unable to speak. Quite a bit for a young father to handle, wouldn't you agree?

But Jesus is coming his way. *Oh well,* the father might have thought. *What can it hurt? We've certainly tried everything else.*

"What's the problem here?" I can almost hear Jesus ask.

"It's my boy," the man responds.

"Oh?" the Master inquires. "What about him?"

Almost embarrassed, the man explains. "I asked your disciples," the man said, his tone dropping almost to a whisper. "But, I guess . . ."

Jesus mutters something the man doesn't understand until He clearly speaks the words "Bring the boy to me."

One can only imagine what the man thought next when the boy was brought toward Jesus. You see, the Bible says the

43

boy didn't get better coming closer, he got worse!

"How long has he been like this?" Jesus asks, turning His attention from the convulsing boy at His feet to the distraught father standing close by.

"All his life," the man sadly admits. "And it's been worse. This thing, whatever it is, has thrown him into the fire, even into water. Trying to kill him." Then his eyes lift from the pitiful figure writhing on the ground to meet those of the Master. "But . . ." he hesitates. "But if you can do anything . . . please take pity on us and help us."

"If?" Jesus responds, still ignoring the boy, focusing instead on his father. "If I can?"

I can almost see Jesus reach out and take the man's elbow and with direct and intense eye contact say, "Everything is possible to him who believes."

"I do believe!" the man enthusiastically exclaims. Then under the penetrating gaze of the Son of God, in a much quieter, honest tone he adds, "Help me overcome my unbelief!"

Only when the man's *unbelief* is confessed does Jesus turn His attention back to the boy being ravaged by the evil spirit. A simple command from Jesus and the boy shakes violently once more. Then, as suddenly as it began, it's over— permanently. The evil spirit has manifested itself in the child for the very last time.

"If you believe . . ." Jesus still says to His followers today.

Will we, like this young father, have the courage to admit that while we believe we still struggle with unbelief when it comes to certain difficult situations? And will we have the wisdom to cry out to Christ at such times and say, "Help me overcome my unbelief"?

If we are to answer the invitation of our loving Savior, Jesus Christ, to come away with Him, we will have to step out of our privately held areas of unbelief. To come away with Him means we will have to step away from our unbelief as a little boy steps out of his dirty clothes before climbing into the bathtub.

But coming away from our unbelief doesn't mean it will go away. Unfortunately it will lie right where we left it, waiting for our return. And some will return. But that would be like the little boy getting right back into his dirty clothes following his bath!

Joyfully, some of us never will step back into our unbelief once we realize how wonderful it is to leave it behind. As the little boy in our scriptural reading received permanent deliverance, and as his father's unbelief was forever banished that day, we too can experience the touch of Jesus Christ at such a level that our unbelief will lie unclaimed until it becomes like so much petrified wood in an ancient forest. Never to live or be active again.

Why? Because we prayed that one simple prayer: "Help me overcome my unbelief."

Can you see yourself as the little boy stepping into his bath? Can you imagine your unbelief lying in an abandoned heap on the floor like so many dirty clothes? Do you realize the luxurious experience of soaking in God's precious, purifying, cleansing river of life?

Consider these words of wisdom:

> Spiritual faith does not come about by saying, "Show me a sign, God. Answer my prayer. Perform a miracle." It begins by believing simply that *God is*—and He is above His creation. "Behold I make new things," says the Word, "which eye has not seen, and ear has not heard, nor has it entered into the heart of man" (1 Corinthians 2:9; Isaiah 64:4). Ask God, therefore, to give you new eyes, new ears, and a new heart. For whatever your human senses insist that you believe *must* be brought under the spirit. Otherwise you will always be under the dominion and control of the flesh and of the world. You will always interpret the events of your life by what your senses tell you, and not by faith.

—Clement of Alexandria, *You Give Me New Life*

Enjoy these words of beauty:

My faith has found a resting place,
Not in device nor creed;
I trust the ever-living One,

45

His wounds for me shall plead.

Enough for me that Jesus saves—
This ends my fear and doubt;
A sinful soul I come to Him,
He'll never cast me out.

My heart is leaning on the Word,
The written Word of God,
Salvation by my Savior's name,
Salvation through His blood.

My great Physician heals the sick,
The lost He came to save;
For me His precious blood He shed,
For me His life He gave.

I need no other argument,
I need no other plea;
It is enough that Jesus died,
And that He died for me.

—Lidie H. Edmunds

How do you think unbelief hinders our relationship with Jesus Christ?

Recall a time when you quickly said, "I believe," then had to back away and admit you needed help overcoming unbelief:

How was that similar to putting dirty clothes back on after a warm, cleansing bath?

How would you verbalize your need to overcome unbelief today?

For what situation?

Write a new or renewed commitment to come away from unbelief here:

Chapter
· 6 ·

Come Alone . . .

Read Matthew 6:5–6.
Reflect on these words from verse 6:

"When you pray, go into your room, close the door . . ."

. . . all by yourself. Nobody else.

"Go to your room!" the parent barks. "Think about what you've done, and I'll be up in a little while to discuss this."

Or, "Go to your room and work on that attitude."

Or how about, "Go to your room and get that homework done!"

All kinds of memories flood back to me when I read these words from Matthew, chapter six. I heard these words as a child; I repeated them as a parent.

Nothing felt as lonely as being banished from the family while I tended to personal issues or behaviors my parents termed unacceptable. If I'm not careful, that's the interpretative spin I will put on this passage.

But God's call isn't punitive; it's an invitation. A personal call for a rendezvous with royalty. An intimate moment with the Master. A chance to share secrets with the Savior. A date for privacy with Jesus himself. A call to a pure hug from Papa God.

And, like all private, intimate moments between two people who love each other, it's not for public display. Bringing someone else along spoils the moment.

However, our lifestyles reveal that rather than cherish moments alone, we avoid them. We've added phones to our cars, sometimes even our bathrooms. We've connected to the World Wide Web and communicate with total strangers, sometimes in preference to thinking our own thoughts. We load our mornings with *Good Morning, America* or *Regis and Kathie Lee* rather than work around our house in solitude. We take our coffee break with friends or co-workers, opting for the company of others. We read newspapers or books on the subway instead of shutting ourselves in for a moment of inner solitude.

Is being alone a lost art? A forgotten discipline? If so, how tragic, for it will certainly have a detrimental effect on our prayer life. For God's Word says, *Go to your room—your private room.* And, it adds, *Close the door and pray to your Father, who is unseen.* Alone? Yes, but not really. God invites, not sends you to solitude. He is there already, waiting. *Then your Father,* the Bible continues, *who sees what is done in secret . . .* This is a meeting of the most private kind.

Remember the mysterious, cloaked figure in the introduction to this section? What if that was God arranging a rendezvous with you? Would you hasten to the appointment? Would you be tempted to take someone along for protection—just in case?

Let's answer His invitation today. Let's hurry to the place of solitude with God. And let's do it joyfully, gladly, willingly. He awaits.

———

Consider these words of wisdom:

> Don't you feel a tug, a yearning to sink down into the silence and solitude of God? Don't you long for something more? Doesn't every breath crave a deeper, fuller exposure to His presence? It is the discipline of solitude that will open the door.

> —Richard J. Foster, *Celebration of Discipline*

Enjoy these words of beauty:

> My lover spoke and said to me, "Arise, my darling,

my beautiful one, and come with me. See! The winter is past; the rains are over and gone. Flowers appear on the earth; the season of singing has come, the cooing of doves is heard in our land. The fig tree forms its early fruit; the blossoming vines spread their fragrance. Arise, come, my darling; my beautiful one, come with me."

—Solomon (Song of Songs 2:10–13)

———

Do you enjoy solitude?

Can you translate any childhood experiences into reasons why you might want to avoid being alone?

Do you have difficulty keeping others out of the times you set aside for solitude? Why?

If you were to set aside a specific time for solitude, when might that time be?

When someone in authority says to you, "May I see you in my office, please?" what immediately runs through your mind?

What emotions do you experience?

What would it take to help you understand that God's invitation is not punitive in purpose?

Do you welcome or avoid emotional intimacy with God? Comment.

Can you see any connection between the last two questions?

What would you like to say to God about that?

Chapter
· 7 ·

The True Me

Read John 4:4–26.
Reflect on these words from verse 18:

"What you have just said is quite true."

It's true. Jesus knows more about who we really are than anyone else—even ourselves.

I know this is true about me. You see, I have many "selves." No, not personalities—*selves*. You see my public self. An area of myself that is known to me and also to others. I have complete control over my public self. I choose which information about me I put out for public display. But I also have a private self. Areas of my inner self that I don't put on public parade. Even more than that, I have a self that my friends see but I don't. My blind spots. I also have a developing self that is still unexplored, either by me or by others— my untapped potential-filled self. It's that way for all of us.

But more than that, I'm aware that I have at least two other selves. A true self and a false self.

The false self is what I have purposely created to present as a favorable imitation of my true self, which only I know is totally false. No kidding. It's that self-made facade I created that remains outwardly calm when inside I'm in rage. The self-made simulation of visible patience when inside I'm screaming with impatience. The nice, self-righteous presentation I make that is loving and nonjudgmental when at the same time I'm yelling inside, "How could you do such a stupid thing?"

One day in our ladies' Bible study at church, we were studying Cynthia Heald's marvelous book *Becoming a Woman of Excellence*. Someone made the comment that there were certain women she was sure never raised their voices in anger, flew off the handle, or demanded their own way. She named several of them and *my name was on that list!* Inside I laughed, but on the outside, I simply smiled and looked at another lady whose name was also on the list— whose smile mirrored mine. I can't speak for my counterpart, but for me it was most revealing. I had managed to create an impression of a mature, calm, peaceful woman. Hardly an accurate or consistent picture of my inner, real self. And, not to my credit, I let the assumption—the false impression— stand. An image my family would scoff at, I'm sure.

You see, I've learned to present my best self in public. I can manage to be a picture of perfect calm when I'm nervous. I can bluff my way with ease in the company of celebrities or even remain totally calm and clearheaded in an emergency, only to fall apart in private later. I can be outgoing and personable, even when I would rather be alone with my rubber-stamping hobby. Only I know the truth.

Don't get me wrong. I'm not presenting a false self every time I appear calm, at ease, outgoing, or personable. Only sometimes. But because I've done such an excellent job with my created, false self, most people would never guess this about me. Only God knows, because, you see, there isn't anything about me He doesn't know.

Not that I'm a counterfeit person, but it's not always appropriate to reveal my true self in public. If I'm speaking, for example, it's not necessary to put my whole unvarnished self on exhibit. People who expect me to provide a message of encouragement and hope and to represent Christ don't have to hear how frustrated I am over a clogged drain, the pimple behind my ear, or how hurt and angry I am at one of my children. I've had to overlook unkind remarks, and even questions that invade my privacy, minutes before standing behind a podium to present the love of Christ.

But when I answer God's call to "come into my room and

shut the door" for intimate moments with Him, it's time to leave behind all but my true self, whether it be my public, private, hidden, or undiscovered true self. This is when I can safely let all the secrets of my heart lay bare. When I come alone, step away from all my "selves," and present only my true self to God, it's wonderful. I don't have to make excuses, hold up a facade, or wear a mask. There is nothing to keep up for appearances' sake, no image at stake or reputation to protect. It's just me—the real, genuine, undecorated, bare-faced me, alone in the presence of my Papa God, who knows me inside and out. Without shame or hesitation I can present my real, true self. It doesn't make any sense for me to embellish myself for somebody I can't impress with impersonations of the real me. He loves me, even without my fancy, false self. What a relief!

Then I discover that something quite amazing begins to happen. My inner self, my true self, presented to Him in a downright, honest way is what He actually begins to touch and change. The true me is the material He uses to help me become more like I really want to be—even more true, more like Christ. The need for my outer, false self actually diminishes and dies. There are more times when I'm as calm on the inside as I am on the outside. On the other hand, there are also more times I have the courage to be as nervous outside as inside. More times when my inner self and outer self match. Why? Because I'm actually losing my fear of being *my true self*!

Yes, you can "come alone" in the sense that you have separated from other people, yet still be in a self-created, self-centered, and self-seeking crowd of your false selves. Won't you try this experiment? Come alone, leave all but your true self on the other side of the closed door while you meet with God at an honest, heart-to-heart level. He'd really like to spend time with you—just your true self, alone.

Wouldn't it be wonderful to pour out your heart to the King of Kings and have Him look with total compassion and love into your eyes and whisper, "What you have just said is quite true."

Consider these words of wisdom:

> Do not misunderstand me; He wants you to live abundantly, but this can only be accomplished by allowing Him to cut into that fleshly part of you that is still stubbornly clinging to life. Don't expect God to deal with those vulgar, wicked desires that you renounced forever when you gave yourself away to Him. That part of you is already dead. But He will deal with the parts of you that are still alive. . . .
>
> You must be willing to yield to the will of God whenever He decides to remove from you all the props on which you have leaned.

—Fenelon, *Let Go*

Enjoy these words of beauty:

> Just as I am, without one plea,
> But that Thy blood was shed for me,
> And that Thou bidd'st me come to Thee,
> O Lamb of God, I come, I come!
>
> Just as I am and waiting not
> To rid my soul of one dark blot,
> To Thee, whose blood can cleanse each spot,
> O Lamb of God, I come, I come!
>
> Just as I am, Thou wilt receive,
> Wilt welcome, pardon, cleanse, relieve;
> Because Thy promise I believe,
> O Lamb of God, I come, I come!
>
> Just as I am, Thy love unknown
> Hath broken every barrier down;
> Now, to be Thine, yea, Thine alone,
> O Lamb of God, I come, I come!

—Charlotte Elliott

What impressions do you most like to leave when meeting somebody new?

How do you carry those same intentions for making a good impression into your private times with God?

What do you think I would think of you if I knew "the real you"?

What do you think God thinks of "the real you"? (Refer to Psalm 139 to see how God really feels about you.)

If you were to lay down your false self, what would have to go?

If you went into your room and closed the door, presenting only your real self before God, what would that mean?

What risks would you have to be willing to take?

Write a short prayer of commitment to bring only your true self when you meet alone with God:

Chapter
· 8 ·

Forming a New Attachment

Read Luke 18:18–30.
Reflect on these words from verse 28:

"We have left all we had to follow you!"

And these words of Jesus from Matthew 10:39:

"Whoever loses his life for my sake will find it."

Attachments, accessories, appendages . . . no matter what I call them, they are the "stuff of life" with which I pad, prop, and pretty up my existence emotionally, physically, and spiritually. Of course, I can add to the list: addictions, approval, achievements, accomplishments, acquisitions, acquaintances, ambitions, abilities, activities—and I haven't even started on the "b's" yet!

This is the stuff of life that Jesus urges His followers to die to. To lose, to leave behind. It is essential to inner solitude.

I like the way Alden E. Sproull, chaplain of Redlands Community Hospital in Redlands, California, says it: "At the root of [the] prayer of the heart is the call of God to become detached from the addictions of life. We may have become addicted to attitudes, beliefs, things, feelings, substances, possessions, and relationships that block our intimacy with Jesus Christ. We soon discover that such attach-

61

ments become idolatry. They have become more important to our sense of wholeness than intimacy with Jesus Christ."*

Reading his article sent me scurrying to read Jesus' words from Matthew 10:39: "Whoever loses his life for my sake will find it."

What addictions or attachments do I have in my life? I wondered. Seeking God at a new level, longing for new quietness and even silence before Him, I want nothing standing between my soul and my Savior. I want no static in the transmissions of love that pass from the Lover of my soul to me. I desire complete intimacy with Christ and yearn for nothing to hinder a deepening relationship with God. I looked inside and what I found wasn't pretty!

With the help of a little *Webster's Word Guide* to prod my thinking, I began with "a" and am presently working my way through the entire alphabet, letting the Holy Spirit highlight words to me as I scan the columns.

Using this simple method, in the span of a month I discovered lots of stuff-of-life attachments I thought I needed or might need someday. Protective emotional gear, excuses, the tendency to cover my back, and lots more negative, self-created padding around my heart. Then I discovered my need for affection, my propensity toward doubt, possessiveness toward my family, and on and on. I'd like to say that I'm done with this process; however, when I looked up the word "lose" in my biblical reference books, I discovered that according to the original Greek, the verb tense used in Matthew 10:39 means "losing"—"Whoever *is losing* his life for my sake . . ." That means even more growth ahead—a continuous, ongoing process! (Ouch! I just discovered pain, performance, and possessions.)

But also ahead of me is the promise of finding more than I ever lost. I actually have hope of discarding old, destructive attachments and enjoying new, pure ones.

When searching out the deep riches of the word "find," I learned that it means to *discover and obtain for myself.* At the same time that Jesus tells me to let go of life, He's offering me a totally new way to live. Instead of a life of self-

*"C'mon, Try Something Old and Different," *Herald of Holiness,* June 1996.

preservation, He offers a life of discovery. Instead of self-edification, a life of exciting exploration. Instead of loss and disappointment, a life defined by such words as *gain* and *obtain*. Instead of failure, a life of progress and productivity.

I don't have to live a life based on me, my wishes, my beliefs, and my urges; I can grab hold of a life based on Him, His will for me, His truth, and His guidance.

I understand more clearly than ever that the invitation to come alone has to include loosening my grip on the stuff of life and hanging on only to Jesus Christ, who *is* Life!

I am enthusiastically answering His adventurous, intriguing invitation. Want to come along? Remember—come alone—lose your "stuff."

————

Consider and enjoy these words of wisdom and beauty:

Nothing between my soul and the Savior,
Naught of this world's elusive dream;
I have renounced all sinful pleasure,
Jesus is mine; There's nothing between.

Nothing between, like worldly pleasure,
Habits of life, though harmless they seem,
Must not my heart from Him ever sever,
He is my all, there's nothing between.

Nothing between, like pride or station,
Self or friends shall not intervene,
Tho' it may cost me much tribulation,
I am resolved, there's nothing between.

Nothing between, e'en many hard trials,
Tho' the whole world against me convene;
Watching with prayer and much self-denial,
I'll triumph at last, with nothing between.

Nothing between my soul and the Savior,
So that His blessed face may be seen;
Nothing preventing the least of His favor,
Keep the way clear! Let nothing between.

—C. A. Tindley

————

Similar to my list in the first paragraph of this chapter, are there any attachments you might have that would prevent you from "coming alone" into the presence of Jesus Christ?

Respond to Chaplain Sproull's words as you apply them to your own life:

How can you further embrace the challenge to "lose your life"?

Practically speaking, what specific things could you possibly need to let go of?

Emotionally?

Physically or materially?

Spiritually?

In losing your life, what new attachments do you hope to make?

What discoveries do you hope to make? What kind of life do you hope to find? Verbalize that hope in a written prayer below:

Chapter · 9 ·

What Kind of Friend Is That?

Read John 15:12–17.
Reflect on these words from verse 13:

"Greater love has no one than this, that one lay down his life for his friends."

When was the last time you wondered if there were any true friends left? Friends that would love you no matter what. Perhaps a special, specific friend who would accept the real, unvarnished, unembellished you.

Someone who would see value in you, even on your worst days. One who could see through your failures to your potential for success still ahead. Somebody to love you in spite of your faults. Is there anybody you know who would actually lay down his or her life for you if push came to shove? Do you know anyone who would go out of his or her way, set aside their own personal interests, or even their identity, for your benefit? And do you know one single person in the whole world who would do such things even if you didn't recognize his or her attempts to win you over or acknowledge their existence?

I have such a friend. And, whether or not you recognize it, you do too. His name is Jesus.

"You did not choose me," He says, "but I chose you . . ." (John 15:16).

He chose you—and even more incomprehensible: He

chose you long before you were even born! (See Jeremiah 1:5.) Long before you were able to create and present your false, impressive selves. He loved your unformed substance, your unaffected personality, your genetic makeup. He loved you, even though He knew you would sin, and because of that He paid your ransom, ready to redeem you the moment you admitted your sinfulness and need of a Savior. He laid down His life for you before you even knew you needed someone to pay such a sacrificial price in your behalf. He loved you, even though He knew you would be persuaded to adorn yourself with unneeded trappings of your culture—even after you became His friend. He loved you, even though He knew you'd believe the worst about yourself, because He saw the best in you. I know this because I have experienced it for myself.

He came to earth to walk through a human life, living among people in much the same way you and I do today. He came to set foot on this planet because there was no other way to reach you. He came to us because there was no way for us to get to Him.

No greater friend, the Bible says. He laid His life down for us. And now it's our turn.

In the previous chapter we read in Matthew 10:39 that in order to find our life in Christ, we must first be willing to lose it.

In the chapter before that we learned that He knows our true selves. And before that we were invited to go into our room and be with Him *behind closed doors.*

In a way, we have been learning what it means to lay down our lives for *Him.* The cost of true friendship with Christ. Does that sound incredible?

Laying down our lives isn't just a message for missionaries, evangelists, or pastors. It's not just for committed marriage partners or parents. It's an invitation we all must hear, confront, and respond to. Jesus invites us all, you and me, to spend time with Him alone. As much as He needed time alone with His Father, so do we.

So today, I have brought you to a threshold. The invitation still stands—come alone.

Pastor's wife, come without your guard up. Working

mother, lay down your demanding schedule. Home-schooling parent, lay aside your responsibility. Doctor, let your patients wait. Teacher, step away from your students. Writer, get away from your keyboard. Single woman, lay aside your self-sufficiency or loneliness. Single mom, put aside the double load you carry. Businesswoman, turn your back on the phone and your prospects. Executive, close your briefcase. Student, walk away from your books.

Abuse victim, know that you can safely walk away from your pain. Abandoned and betrayed one, believe that you can trust Him. Wandering soul, come home. Emotionally injured one, don't be afraid; He won't hurt you.

Your Best-Friend-Ever awaits. And He invites—come alone. In order to answer His invitation, simply picture yourself standing at the threshold of a room, then walking unhindered and free, laying down your life, your past, your responsibilities, and your multiple selves—leaving them in the hallway. Enter in, enjoy His presence. Be a friend to Him, as He is to you.

Consider these words of wisdom:

> Christ comes only in secret to those who have entered the inner chamber of the heart and closed the door.

> —Thomas Merton, *Contemplative Prayer*

Enjoy these words of beauty:

> Out of my bondage, sorrow and night,
> Jesus, I come, Jesus, I come;
> Into Thy freedom, gladness and light,
> Jesus, I come to Thee;
> Out of my sickness into Thy health,
> Out of my want and into Thy wealth.
> Out of my sin and into Thyself,
> Jesus, I come to Thee.

Out of my shameful failure and loss,
Jesus, I come, Jesus, I come;
Into the glorious gain of Thy cross,
Jesus, I come to Thee;
Out of earth's sorrows into Thy balm,
Out of life's storms and into Thy calm,
Out of distress to jubilant psalm,
Jesus, I come to Thee.

Out of unrest and arrogant pride,
Jesus, I come, Jesus, I come.
Into Thy blessed will to abide,
Jesus, I come to Thee;
Out of myself to dwell in Thy love,
Out of despair into raptures above,
Upward for aye on wings like a dove,
Jesus, I come to Thee.

Out of the fear and dread of the tomb,
Jesus, I come, Jesus, I come;
Into the joy and light of my home,
Jesus, I come to Thee;
Out of the depths of ruin untold,
Into the peace of Thy sheltering fold,
Ever Thy glorious face to behold,
Jesus, I come to Thee.

—William T. Sleeper

What thoughts, fears, or distractions do you need to deal with in order to answer Christ's invitation to come alone?

What are some creative places that would accommodate your being alone with Christ for a while?

What are the best times for you to "come alone"?

What are the worst times for you to try to be alone?

Write an "R.S.V.P. prayer" to Christ's invitation to come alone here:

Chapter
· 10 ·

Appointed to Go, Anointed to Love

Read again John 15:12–17.
Reflect on these words found in verse 16:

> "*I chose you and appointed you to go and bear fruit—fruit that will last.*"

And verse 17:

> "*This is my command: Love each other.*"

I have two great friends who are so different they have nothing in common with each other except me. They have different personalities, lifestyles, and needs. If they attended the same church and didn't know me, they probably wouldn't choose each other as close friends. Yet on the occasions when we all get together, they treat each other with great respect and friendliness. Their joined laughter is very satisfying to me. Their combined sense of humor is joyful. These two women hold quite different church and doctrinal beliefs, and each have expressed totally different opinions when I've asked for their advice. Yet when we are together, they meet on common ground. How can they be so congenial and loving toward each other? Because of me. I want my friends to be friends with all my other friends. If for no other reason than that I love them both so very much. And so it is with Jesus.

Unless you are called and gifted to live the cloistered, monastic life, His call to solitude, being alone with Him, isn't to be lived apart, excluding others for long periods of time. His invitation to come away, come alone, is followed by His command to *go*. Go and love. In other words, when we are called to be His friend, we are then commissioned to be a friend to all His other friends.

You left your self-life with its false selves, unneeded attachments, and addictions at the door, remember? Now you are called to leave this place of solitude and go and love—but be careful to step over or go around the place where you left those other self-created, stuff-of-life props. No need to pick them up again, for you will just have to go through the process of laying them down again when you return to your time alone with Jesus.

Rather, let them lie there unattended while you go about loving Jesus' other friends. Friends like your family, your neighbors, and the people at work. Friends like the people at church, those who attend your Bible study, or sing in the choir with you.

You see, the amazing thing is that when you spend moments of solitude with the Savior, you can actually take the fruit of that solitude—His peace—with you as you obey His command to go. The inner solitude of His wonderful presence can fill those places left empty by ridding your soul of self. He can now flood your inner self with His peace, His presence, and His love. That's why He can trust you to go and love—because it's His love you are to take with you and spread around for others to enjoy.

Today, after I finish writing this, I have an opportunity to do something for one of His friends. Moments ago, it was just Jesus and me—suddenly it becomes Jesus and *we*. Community, networking, whatever the current buzz word, it really means family. Alone with Christ never leads me to loneliness—but to love.

So what are you waiting for? Go and love somebody!

———

Consider these words of wisdom:

74

The life that Jesus brings is a shared life. The life of God in the world does not have its meaning in isolated units, but in a fellowship of those who share that life in Him.

—Reuben Welch, *We Really Do Need Each Other*, Zondervan Publishers, 1982 (from *Impact*; 1973)

Enjoy these words of beauty:

A friend of Jesus, O what bliss,
That one so vile as I
Could ever have a friend like this
To lead me to the sky.

A friend when other friendships cease,
A friend when others fail,
A friend who gives me joy and peace,
A friend when foes assail.

A friend when sickness lays me low,
A friend when death draws near,
A friend as through the vale I go,
A friend to help and cheer.

A friend when life's short race is o'er,
A friend when earth is past,
A friend to meet on heaven's shore,
A friend when home at last.

Friendship with Jesus,
Fellowship divine,
O what blessed sweet communion,
Jesus is a friend of mine.

—Major Ludgate

How has your definition of "coming alone" changed since you began this section of the book?

In the past, how have you resisted being alone with God?

What changes have you made so far as a result of this study?

What difficulties have you encountered up to this point?

If you were to write a new or renewed commitment to answer God's call to quiet, what would you say?

Section III

———

Come Quietly

BY THE AGE OF FIVE, my son had developed the irritating habit of walking into a room talking. It didn't matter if I was on the phone or talking to one of his sisters—he simply expected me to be there waiting for him. Perhaps he thought I had nothing else to do but wait for him to tell me something. It took years to break that interruptive habit.

Sometimes prayer life is very similar. Even before I sit down for my prayer time, I'm rehearsing my prayer requests. I don't want to forget anything and, with my crowded schedule, goodness knows I don't have time to revisit my quiet time once I've begun my busy day. Rushing in, I blurt out my wants, needs, and wishes—as if God were simply waiting on pins and needles for me and my list!

My daughter, on the other hand, had a way of coming up beside me, slipping her little arm around my waist, and just waiting quietly for me to turn my attention to her. When she was smaller, she hugged my leg and waited. Many times all she wanted was closeness, love. Just to be near me seemed to be enough.

That's how I really want my prayer time to be—confidently slipping into the throne room, standing close enough to God to embrace Him, and waiting in His presence. Just to be near is enough.

How about you? Have you ever prepared an organized prayer list as so many notes to take to a business meeting? In other words, when it comes to prayer do you "enter the room talking"? Or, like my daughter, do you take the time to approach God quietly? Sometimes for nothing more than to be with Him?

Prayer is more than having God's ear. It's not like taking

78

a number at the local bakery or catalog order department. It is not only our appointment with Him but His time with us. Prayer is more, much more, than our talking to God. Prayer is also *being* in His presence, being with Him, and His being with us—and loving each other.

God is not like a doctor with a ten-minute limit per patient. He's not like a pastor with a waiting room full of people to see after you leave. He's not like the drive-thru at a fast-food restaurant, taking your order through a microphone in the middle of a blessing-of-the-day menu board and handing out answers at the window as you pull up. He's not like the woman at your church, all smiles and friendly while looking over your shoulder to see if anyone more interesting or socially acceptable is around.

When you come quietly into God's presence, you have His full attention from the beginning. Even if you sit without saying a word for half an hour or more, you will still have His full listening ear. Your prayers can't attract more attention than He's already given you. You don't have to entertain Him or convince Him of your need. You don't have to keep your agenda moving or lose Him to someone else. He is totally there, fully alert, completely centered on you for as long as you wish.

Don't discount the importance and deep personal meaning of silent times with God. Don't make the mistake of underestimating your own importance to Him or doubt His willingness to spend a quiet time with you.

His invitation includes coming to Him in quiet—to quiet. To share in His presence, receive His peace, and experience His love. Just to be together. Side by side, sometimes in silence.

When you answer His call to quiet . . . try not to enter the room talking.

Chapter · 11 ·

It's About Time

Read Ecclesiastes 3:1–8.
Reflect on these words from verses 1 and 7:

There is a time for everything . . . a time to be silent. . . .

Years, seasons, months, weeks, days, hours, minutes, seconds—because we can divide time into measurable increments, we sometimes think we can increase it, that with a great deal of personal effort and discipline we can "save" time. We say that by being patient we are "giving" ourselves time. We juggle appointments, activities, and events, kidding ourselves into thinking we are "making" time. By procrastination we think we are "buying" time, as if it were a tangible commodity. We think in terms of wasting time, passing time, and managing time.

But the truth of it is, in the midst of what Gordon MacDonald describes in his book *Restoring Your Spiritual Passion* as "an enlarging schedule, events and commitments seemingly out of control, and calendars jammed with good things to do," if we are ever to discover, experience, and benefit from quiet in God's blessed presence, it will be because we *take* time. Make a firm appointment to meet with God in quiet.

Scripture teaches that such times are not only appropriate, but biblically ordained—even today, in our fast-paced modern existence. Right in the middle of our busy, noisy world, it is in our best interest to make a habit of taking time for silence—yes, silence.

If there is anything more uncomfortable in our current action-packed, people-and-performance-oriented lifestyle than solitude, it is silence.

We rush into our quiet homes, turn on the radio or TV, or stack several CDs into the stereo. We fill our homes and offices with sounds of music, news, or talk-shows. We give precious hours to channel surfing, scanning hundreds of program offerings by remote control. Finding nothing to catch and hold our attention, we slip a video into the VCR. Through entertainment we make every effort to occupy our minds and pacify our souls, accepting shallow substitutes for the peace of mind and quietness of heart for which we truly hunger. All the while we starve ourselves mentally, emotionally, and spiritually. Furthermore, while we fill our immediate environment with noise, we rob ourselves of passion and guarantee deep inner exhaustion. We hunger for silence.

How about you? Are you tired of listening to the exhausting sounds of life? Are you hungering for the sweet sounds of silence for a change? Maybe it's time—a time for silence.

This week, why not let yourself feel the hunger for silence? Listen to the emptiness in your soul that only quietness can satisfy. Then declare a "noise fast" as a sacrifice unto the Lord. Ask Him to restore you in the joy and strength of quiet. Let the peace of quietness once again refresh your spirit.

At first, start with five minutes. Five solid, wonderful, purposeful minutes of absolute silence. No noise going in, no words coming out. Push the limit to ten minutes, then fifteen, and eventually move to twenty or more minutes of blessed, peace-filled quietness. You'll be surprised what you will hear deep within the noise of stillness, the sounds of silence, the peace of quiet.

Isn't it time? Yes, surely it is—a time for silence.

———————

Consider these words of wisdom:

82

The only answer to an exhausted, passionless life is to check the condition of the subsurface, the inner spirit. That's where the Sabbath, the *still time* comes in.

—Gordon MacDonald, *Restoring Your Spiritual Passion*

Enjoy these words of beauty:

Blessed quietness, holy quietness—
What assurance in my soul!
On the stormy sea,
He speaks to me.
How the billows cease to roll!

—Manie Payne Ferguson

Examine, then list the habits of noise that you have established in your daily life:

Can you think of why you have filled your life with such noise?

Spend five minutes in total silence, then consider the following:

What are the inner noises that prevent silence from being enjoyable? Guilt? Fear? Loneliness?

What external arrangements will you have to make to encourage a successful "noise fast"? Get up earlier? Trim back activities? Say "no" once in a while? Other:

What internal issues or voices need to be silenced to enhance future "noise fasts"?

Chapter · 12 ·

God's Getting Up!

Read Zechariah 2:1–13.
Reflect on these words from verse 13:

"Be still before the LORD, all mankind, because he has roused himself from his holy dwelling."

Zechariah watches in horror as sin and religious indifference spread like influenza, infecting God's people. Lifting his voice like a civil defense siren before a tornado touch down, the young man shouts his prophetic warning. In the third of eight prophetic visions, he summons God's people with these words from Zechariah 2:13: "He has roused himself. . . ."

One can only imagine the sudden hush of heaven when the Divine Creator and Ruler of all things rises from His throne and thrusts out His arms in sweeping magnificence. Can you picture it? Great hosts of angels freeze in midair. Cherubim instantly motionless, the "great cloud of witnesses" hush their praises and wait in awe. Who wouldn't fall at His feet in adoration and worship? One simple command and planets would be paralyzed in their orbits, the earth's rotation brought to an abrupt halt. Yet we know it isn't the created mass of earth and stone that is summoned to stillness, it is us—you and I.

No matter what you carry today, no matter how busy or overloaded your schedule, hear and answer the call to stillness before Him. Whatever denies you peace, demands your attention, and saps your strength, listen and obey His call to quiet.

Let this word of the prophet Zechariah be delivered personally to you today. Hear the word of the Lord calling you: *Be still.* That's right, in the middle of your struggle, in spite of whatever pain and discomfort you may be experiencing, God is calling you to stillness before Him. Regardless of your pressured schedule, the challenge of unresolved conflict or pending decision, He calls you to quiet. How will you answer?

God has roused himself—let us be still before Him!

———

Consider these words of wisdom:

> Solitude is the place where the whole of our personality and being, seen and unseen, is drawn together in the transforming presence of God's love. But more than that, the silence of solitude is the silence of eternity.

—David Runcorn, *A Center of Quiet*

Enjoy these words of beauty:

> God of our strength, enthroned above,
> The source of life, the fount of love;
> O let devotion's sacred flame
> Our souls awake to praise Thy name.

> God of our strength, from day to day
> Direct our thoughts and guide our way;
> O may our hearts united be
> In sweet communion, Lord, with Thee.

—Frances Jane Van Alstyne

———

If you were physically present to witness God rising from His throne and summoning all to silence, how do you think you'd respond?

Chapter
· 13 ·

Unfilling the
Silence

Read Isaiah 30:15–18.
Reflect on these words from verse 15:

*"In quietness and trust is your strength, but you would have
none of it."*

Why do we fight against silence? It's a probing question
I've been asking myself lately. Why, when I have the perfect
place, a good reason, and plenty of opportunity, do I resist
being quiet before the Lord? Why do I find every excuse to
do something else? What is behind my resistance? Is silence
that awkward and uncomfortable? Yes, I must admit it is.

You see, when I come to God with an intercessor's call
and burden, I can get right to the work of prayer. I know the
agenda and can move into activity that is known and familiar. I enter the throne room, deserving to be there because I have a commission from the Lord: a prayer assignment gives me a reason to be with the Father.

When I come into His presence in Bible reading and
praise, devotional activity ushers me into His presence as if
such discipline gives me the right to be there. I know what
to do. I "devote": as a verb—something to do.

And when I come into His presence in worship, certainly
I have the credentials to be there, because I'm no longer simply me, I'm a *worshiper*—officially. It's for Him, after all, not
me. I know what to do: I worship.

89

But in silence? Inactivity? With no other agenda than to be in His presence? With nothing to pray or talk to Him about? What happens if He chooses to speak to me? What if He chooses to be silent? What if He looks at me and sees clear through to my empty, aching heart? What if He sees my lack of faith—tucked away safely out of sight? The anger I have carefully covered? The resentment I secretly harbor against one of His children? What if He sees the pain of the past that I still carry? And what if He chooses to address issues of my character, or my lack of direction?

Certainly it is wonderful and appropriate to worship God. But are we to avoid silence because personal issues might be exposed and addressed? I can choose to fill the silence with songs, praise, prayers, and other "godly" activities. But sooner or later I will have to admit, sometimes it's the very activity of worship that fills the silence. You see, it isn't being with God that makes me squirm; it's being with *me*! And, I must secretly confess, part of me believes that if God really knew me, He wouldn't want to be with me either.

In silence, it's also easy to feel unproductive. There are writing deadlines, new proposals to create and record, church responsibilities, family matters, correspondence, prayers waiting to be prayed, housework to be done—can I afford even a few minutes of silence and inactivity? I realize how much of my sense of worth is related to what I *do* rather than to who I *am*. What I can accomplish rather than who I can become.

How about you? Do you recognize your own reaction to being quiet before God in my confession? Are we very different?

Close to feeling nonproductive is feeling out of control— as if God puts items and assignments into our hands to work out all by ourselves, then holds us personally accountable for their success or failure.

Being quiet in God's presence makes us vulnerable. In our day, vulnerability is akin to being taken advantage of, invaded, and abused. Do we avoid being quiet in God's presence because we are afraid He might do the same?

All the reasons we manufacture for avoiding, resisting, and fleeing His presence are the precise reasons we need to reverse our direction and, instead of running away, run *into* His presence in quietness. The very issues we use to stay away are exactly why we ought to press in.

Silence is not only where we discover our unworthiness but where we discover His worthiness offered unreservedly. Although we can never merit such a privileged appointment, His merit is why we come. Not by anything we have done, but by what He has done. Not because of our credentials, but because of His.

Silence forces us to lay down the busyness of our lives, even doing God's work. It pries us away from accomplishments and makes us aware of our utter helplessness. It's where we are made painfully aware that apart from Him we can do nothing—that we are nothing. But also that *through* Him we can do all things. That *in* Him we are everything we need to be—and more!

Silence loosens the hold on having to be in control. It urges us to let go, to lay down oversized, self-appointed responsibilities and self-inflicted standards of perfection and unreal expectations.

––––––––

Consider these words of wisdom:

> This was the secret of Jesus' life. This was where He found strength to follow the Father's will. When we follow Him we must copy not only His words and actions, but His silence and moments of solitary withdrawing as well. If Jesus needed those times, then we certainly need them more! Like the disciples we follow Him into the desert places. And in our turn, we must learn from Him how to be alone and still.

> —David Runcorn, A *Center of Quiet*

Enjoy these words of beauty:

When the cares of life sweep o'er me,
And my heart with grief is torn,
When I steal away and find a place to pray,
Then Jesus speaks and hope anew is born.

Every day brings some new burden,

And my faith is sorely tried;
But the shadows flee when Jesus speaks to me,
As to the secret place I turn aside.

When the sun of joy is shining,
And the day is bright and fair,
In communion sweet I tarry at His feet
And tell Him how I love to meet Him there.

O Jesus, in the hour of sweet communion
There is rest from every earthly care;
There are depths of love and peace like heav'n above
When Jesus meets the soul in prayer.

—James U. Reid

What religious practices do you use to convince yourself you *deserve* to be in God's presence?

What form of worship do you hold to that *qualifies* you to meet with God?

How can such religious practices, disciplines, or forms of worship stand in the way of truly experiencing God in silence?

Do you hesitate to be any of the following, even in God's presence?

___ vulnerable   ___ out of control   ___ unproductive
___ totally real   ___ transparent   ___ other: _____

To find out why, finish this sentence:

I hesitate to be in silence before God because . . .

What does that reveal?

___ fear   ___ lack of trust   ___ blind spot
___ room for growth ___ need for healing ___ other: _____

Write a prayer about this new insight:

Dear Lord,
    I bring to you my _____ (from list above) and ask
you to help me . . .

Chapter
· 14 ·

Coming to Quiet

Reread Isaiah 30:15–18.
Reflect again on these words from verse 15:

"In quietness and trust is your strength."

Being silent before God isn't easy in this noisy, earthly existence, but it is essential. We have relegated silence, contemplative prayer, and meditation to those who have chosen a monastic lifestyle, who live outside the bounds of what we consider a "normal" existence. But in our noisy world, we too need to set aside regular times for silent contemplation so that the world's noise and clamor does not drown out God's voice within us. We cannot afford to leave to chance the experience of silence and only embrace it at brief, widely spaced intervals in our busy lives.

Have we lost touch with the eloquent sounds of silence and quiet spirituality? Have we lost our appreciation for the beauty of silent moments and quiet experiences altogether?

I am convinced we don't have to be victimized by such a noise-polluted existence—we can learn to still our hearts before God and experience Him in new and wonderfully quiet ways. Even in our overly noisy world we can spend much needed time in silence before the Holy One, who, in direct contrast to the blasting, blustering voices of our day, continues to speak in a still, small voice.

Isaiah 30:15 says, "This is what the Sovereign LORD, the

Holy One of Israel, says: 'In repentance and rest is your salvation, in quietness and trust is your strength. . . . ' " Who among us hasn't clung to that verse at one time or another? " 'But,' " the Lord goes on to say in this passage, " 'you would have none of it.' " Is the last phrase of that passage true of us today? Is it true of you?

For the last several days, we have taken the time to learn to still our souls, to be quiet in God's presence—an important step toward learning to listen. Though this concept of coming before the Lord in silence is not complicated, it may have been difficult for you. Before we make it impossibly complex, let's return to the *simplicity* of silence.

Remember the image of a child presenting a bouquet of flowers to a king? It's something we've all seen, at least on television, or captured by a photojournalist. The little girl steps forward, for a brief moment curtsies, bowing gracefully, her head tipped forward. A memorable, quiet acknowledgment of her honored but humble place before royalty. It's a magic moment, just before she extends her colorful floral gift, when she simply says quietly, "Your Majesty."

In quietness of heart and humility of spirit, we too can bow before the King of Kings. We're invited to enjoy the presence of Jehovah, Almighty Father, our own Papa God. But before we present our gifts of praise, our petitions of prayer, let us simply stop, letting the silence of the moment bring the reality of His Royalty and the realization of our adoption deep into our souls.

Come, He whispers, *Come . . .*

Let us seize this wonderful moment and, in quiet submission, bow low before our Father King and whisper, "Your Majesty!"

Linger in the moment, captured by His attention, locked in the love in His eyes. Savor the privacy, embrace the intimacy of the sacred silence. Bowing before His Majesty let the realization of your rebirth flood you with wonder, let your love for Him flow freely in this exquisite moment. Uttering a single word will break the spell. Hush . . . this moment is not to be rushed.

Consider these words of wisdom:

> More than all, love silence; it brings you a fruit that tongue cannot describe. In the beginning we have to force ourselves to be silent. But then there is born something that draws us to silence. May God give you an experience of the "something" that is born of silence. If only you practice this, untold light will dawn on you in consequence . . . after a while a certain sweetness is born in the heart of this exercise and the body is drawn almost by force to remain in silence.

> —Isaac of Nineveh, Syrian monk
> (Quoted by Thomas Merton,
> *Contemplative Prayer*)

Enjoy these words of beauty:

My Father is rich in houses and lands,
He holdeth the wealth of the world in His hands!
Of rubies and diamonds, of silver and gold,
His coffers are full—He has riches untold.

My Father's own Son, the Savior of men,
Once wandered o'er earth as the poorest of them;
But now He is reigning forever on high,
And will give me a home in heav'n by and by.

I once was an outcast stranger on earth,
A sinner by choice and an alien by birth;
But I've been adopted, my name's written down—
An heir to a mansion, a robe, and a crown.

A tent or a cottage, why should I care?
They're building a palace for me over there!
Though exiled from home, yet still I may sing:
All glory to God, I'm a child of the King!

I'm a child of the King, a child of the King!
With Jesus my Savior, I'm a child of the King!

—Harriett E. Buell

Can you remember a bad experience with an authority figure, such as a parent or schoolteacher, in which you were forced to remain silent? Comment.

How does being silent before God differ from an experience like the one mentioned above?

What changes have you made in your quiet time since studying the concept of silence before God?

How is being quiet easier for you now than when you first began thinking about this concept?

What obstacles still stand in your way?

What prayer would you like to pray about that? Write it here:

Chapter · 15 ·

Be Still and Know...

Read Psalm 46.
Reflect on these words from verse 10:

"Be still, and know that I am God."

Be still . . .
"I can do it myself!" The little girl tugs at the long, unruly laces.
"Better let me," the gentle mother urges.
"I can do it!" the self-confident child insists.
Mother watches, patiently waiting for the inevitable. Sneakers are one thing, but ice skates are quite a different challenge for such a small person. The predictable happens: soon the child is in tears, agitated with her uncooperative and confusing skate laces. Fussing with frustration she kicks the rebellious skate off her foot and folds her arms in angry defiance across her chest.
"Want me to help?" Mother asks.
The angry child nods and Mother reaches for the skate. Once she's begun, little fingers intrude, trying once again to take on the task alone.
"Be still!" Mother instructs. "I will do it, but you'll have to let go."
How many times I've said those words to my children! It's so hard to do things for a stubborn, independent child.
But are children the only ones who insist on maintaining

control when they should let go? Are they the only ones who proclaim their self-sufficiency, even when they are struggling and doomed to failure?

After all, we convince ourselves, the situation demands that somebody do something! Decisions must be made, problems must be solved. Challenges must be met and mature adults don't run away—they stand and face it, even fight if necessary. God gave me a brain; He expects me to use it! Performance-based religion, rather than spirit-experienced relationship, traps us into overestimating the importance of self-sufficient *doing* and tragically underestimating the significance of faith-building *releasing*.

How many times I can look back through the difficulties, crises, and major decisions of my life and see that in the end I had to let go and let God work on my behalf. Even after all my efforts to control things, trying to manage on my own, eventually I had no better choice than to be still—to let go of the situation. Even after serving God for more than forty years, I must admit it still takes attentive effort to slacken my hold, cease my struggling, and *be still*—purposely acknowledging that He is my first resource, not my last resort.

. . . *and know* . . .

Knowing God *can* do it is not the same as being totally convinced and confident that He *will*. Knowing God can meet my need, can answer my prayers, and can touch my pain often remains unseen reality unless I, in stillness, loosen my grip, give up control, and surrender my expectations and demands. In other words, it's only when I let go that I see what God can and will do.

Risky? To stubborn self, most definitely. Foolish? Most assuredly *not*. When is it ever foolish to trust the One who loves us more than we love ourselves? The One who knows the end from the beginning? To depend on His eternal perspective rather than our limited point of view? When would it ever be a risk to give control of our life with its challenges, decisions, and choices to the One who controls the vastness of all creation, and who gave His life for me, then *to* me? Isn't His wisdom far greater than mine? His power beyond my own limited ability? Doesn't He have my best interests at heart, and can't He be trusted to show me the path not only to success but wholeness?

"Stop wiggling," the Scripture says to me. "Stop struggling. Let go. *Be still.*"

"Then," the Holy Spirit whispers into my soul, "and only then, you'll know that I am God. You'll see for yourself only when you stop trying to be your own god. Only then will you finally know me instead."

Jeremiah 9:23–24 puts it like this:

> This is what the LORD says: "Let not the wise man boast of his wisdom or the strong man boast of his strength or the rich man boast of his riches, but let him who boasts boast about this: that he understands and knows me, that I am the LORD, who exercises kindness, justice and righteousness on earth, for in these I delight," declares the LORD.

> Let us be still, and finally, without a doubt, know . . . *He is God!*

Consider these words of wisdom:

> Precisely because the Lord is present with us, we can relax and let go of everything, for in his presence nothing really matters, nothing is of importance except attending to him. We allow inner distractions and frustrations to melt away before him as snow before the sun. We allow him to calm the storms that rage within by saying, "Peace be still." We allow his great silence to still our noisy hearts.

> —Richard Foster,
> *Prayer, Finding the Heart's
> True Home*

Enjoy these words of beauty:

> All to Jesus I surrender,
> All to Him I freely give;
> I will ever love and trust Him,
> In His presence daily live.

All to Jesus I surrender,
Humbly at His feet I bow,
Worldly pleasures all forsaken,
Take me, Jesus, take me now.

All to Jesus I surrender,
Make me, Savior, wholly Thine;
Let me feel the Holy Spirit,
Truly know that Thou art mine.

All to Jesus I surrender,
Lord, I give myself to Thee;
Fill me with Thy love and power,
Let Thy blessing fall on me.

I surrender all, I surrender all.
All to Thee, my blessed Savior, I surrender all.

—Judson W. Van de Venter

———————

How do you finally recognize those times when you are struggling in your own power to accomplish that which you should surrender to God?

If you were to be more aware of God and His working in your life, what would you have to surrender?

In Psalm 46:10 the words *be still* mean more than just "holding oneself quietly"; they also mean "letting go." How does that definition change the way you view your most difficult problem?

In that same verse, the word *and* means "then." How does that change the meaning of this verse for you?

The word *know* means "so see for yourself." What difference does that make to you regarding this remarkable verse?

Read the verse again with these insights and definitions in mind. Write your response in a prayer here:

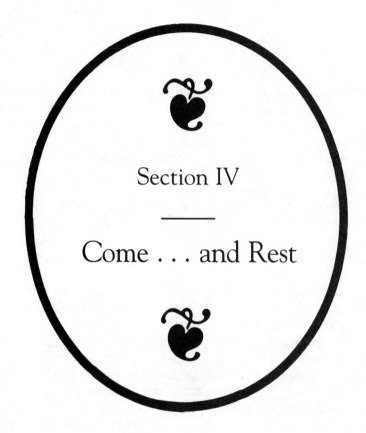

Section IV

———

Come . . . and Rest

BUSYNESS, noise, pressures, decisions. Crowded schedules leave little time for quiet, solitude, and personal space. But are you taking a few minutes each day—reading this book, contemplating its proposals, and considering the questions at the end of each reading? Perhaps this exercise will show you that you can find time and space for some quiet. It may not always be easy, but possible.

I further challenge you to explore your need for *rest*. To look for ways to incorporate it into your daily life. Not away from your crowded life, but in the small spaces and places *within* your life. To make rest a life-saving, life-restoring habit.

The fast-paced whirl of contemporary life often requires high energy levels while leaving no room for rest. Your body screams for you to stop, but instead of taking much-needed rest, you gulp another cup of coffee or swallow an herbal energy booster. A good night's sleep doesn't seem adequate. Long walks in the park or country require too much effort, and you dream of relaxing in a hammock at the beach or among tall pines in the mountains.

In this section, I will encourage you to take another approach to getting the rest you need. It's all part of God's call to quiet—and I am confident you will answer.

Chapter
· 16 ·

"And Now,
a Word
From Our
Sponsor . . ."

Read Mark 6:30–32.
Reflect on these words from verse 31:

"Come . . . and get some rest."

You'll know what I'm talking about. At a high point of intrigue and suspense in a TV drama, when your attention is completely captured, a commercial rudely interrupts: "For acid indigestion and the all-over sick feeling that usually accompanies eating or drinking too much, you need . . ." It's one of the most irritating yet unavoidable modern-day interruptions—a word from your sponsor. Grabbing the remote control, you might push the mute button. They can take away your programming, give you medical, social, and material advice, but they can't make you listen!

Jesus' words in Mark 6:30–31 could be interpreted as such an interruption. The disciples are running high on energy and enthusiasm. Worn out but ready for more. There have been miracles, new converts, and answers to their prayers everywhere they've gone. Tired but excited, they hurry to tell Jesus all about it.

Can you imagine their joy as they rush toward Him, all talking at once? But before they can get it all out, Jesus holds up a hand for silence. "Wait," He says, "you need a rest."

Back off. Take a break. Catch your breath.

Their responses were no doubt as varied as their personalities. Some were glad for the chance to sit down and gather their wits before they gave their report. Others were probably saying, "What? Rest? You must be kidding! Don't you realize the opportunities out there? Everywhere we turn there are people in need. We can't rest now—that would be self-centered, selfish, unthinkable. We're givers; we're in this for you, Lord. As long as we can stand up, we'll keep going. We can rest later."

Recognize yourself here? I do.

For too many of us, with loose ends dangling, decisions to be made, and calendars packed to capacity, taking a step back from our busy lives is unthinkable, too. Momentum would be lost. It would take far too much energy and precious time to get it back again. Yet, knowing all this, the Master's invitation to us is the same: *Come with me . . . get some rest.*

"But," we protest, "if I unwind, how will I ever get *rewound?*"

Or we may complain, "Time out? For what? Life is too short! Every minute counts. Opportunity waits for no one."

Maybe you'd say, "Relax? Not me! I'm just getting started!"

But Jesus' words are not a question, nor are they a negotiable request. They are a gentle command. Not a reminder, not a nudge, but a statement backed by authority. A word from our Sponsor! He isn't interrupting our life or our work. He is showing us *more* of it. He expects us, like His disciples, to take a little time now and then simply to rest. To punctuate our busy lives and important responsibilities with intermissions of repose. To create necessary intervals in our schedules for recesses of quiet.

He took His disciples off the treadmill of their newly discovered gifts and budding ministries for a moment of rest. Out of the fast lane, driven by the needs of those around them, to a relaxing boat ride across the lake. They needed it, and so do you and I.

That's what this book is about. Hearing His call and *not* pressing the mute button. But listening, then getting away

110

with Him for moments of rest and quiet. Not for long. This isn't about getting alone for the weekend and cramming this material into your mind, then rushing back into the busyness of your pressured life. Rather, it's about some much-needed daily breaks, little recesses, time-outs—with Him. To listen to the voice of our Sponsor. Spaces of rest that don't rob you of your momentum, but balance it. This kind of rest isn't intended to make you forget your responsibilities but to face them—whole, refreshed, and renewed.

Take some moments to read this book, think about the questions, and write your answers. Answer God's call to quiet by taking some time to reflect—not to abandon your busy, noisy life altogether, not to desert your duty or neglect your responsibilities, but to gather a bit of quiet that you can take back into the mainstream of your active, productive schedule. The kind of quiet that impacts your entire life and ministry.

Come away, Jesus calls, *and get some rest.* A pause with a purpose. *Step away, pull back.* Answer the call. I can almost picture Him nodding and smiling His affirmation.

Consider these words of wisdom:

> Jesus punctuated his life with silence and solitude. His times alone were the commas, pauses and full stops in the story of his life. They gave the rest of his life its structure, direction and balance. His words and his works were born out of those hours of silent waiting upon God.
>
> —David Runcorn,
> A Center of Quiet

Enjoy these words of beauty:

> My soul, in sad exile, was out on life's sea,
> So burdened with sin and distressed,
> Till I heard a sweet voice saying,
>   "Make me your choice,"
> And I entered the haven of rest.

111

I yielded myself to His tender embrace,
And, faith taking hold of the Word,
My fetters fell off, and I anchored my soul—
The haven of rest is my Lord.

I've anchored my soul in the haven of rest,
I'll sail the wide seas no more;
The tempest may sweep o'er the wild, stormy deep—
In Jesus I'm safe evermore.

—H. L. Gilmour

_____

What is the strongest item or issue in your life that tugs you *away* from taking regular moments of quietness and rest with the Lord?

How could these items or issues benefit from what David Runcorn calls the "structure, direction and balance" that comes from rest?

What demands in your life prevent you from maintaining the discipline necessary for regular intervals of devotion and rest?

What responsibilities will you need to allow to wait, until you've answered God's call to quiet on a more regular basis?

If God's call to quietness and rest has a purpose, what purpose do you think that is for you?

Further thoughts or prayers?

Chapter · 17 ·

The Pause That Refreshes

Read Psalm 23.
Reflect on these words from Exodus 33:14:

"My Presence will go with you, and I will give you rest."

Sometimes I find myself acting as though I believe something that deep down I know is untrue. This is not on purpose, of course, but somehow I slip, perhaps by habit, into either of these two postures:

First, into one that acts as though God is present only in my work, my ministry, or carrying out my responsibilities. I plug along faithfully until I'm so worn out and tired I desperately need a break. When I can go no further, burned out and creatively blocked, I finally stop to catch my breath. But while I'm on my recess, I feel guilty and alone. Cut off from God, I begin to look for another project or activity to return me to His presence.

When I do that, I don't get the rest I need but simply make a change: shifting a heavy burden from one shoulder to the other. I might stop writing for a while but take on new leadership responsibility at church. Using a different set of "muscles" rests the overused ones but not the whole tired, worn-out me. In other words, I'm too tired to do *this* any longer but maybe I could do *that.* This is a performance-based relationship, not a relationship-based performance. Furthermore, it doesn't work. Eventually, I find myself at odds with what I think is an overload from God. Why would He do this to me? The truth is, He doesn't. I do it to myself.

Second, I can entrap myself with an opposite but equally mistaken point of view that says I do my work independently of God's presence: acting as though He is with me and in my quiet times but I'm on my own when it comes to my work, ministry, or responsibilities. That is, I go to Him for recharging but leave Him again when I do His work. Have you ever watched a boxing match and noticed how the fighter has a few last words with his trainer and coach before facing his opponent? After three minutes in the ring, he's back in the corner again, bruised and bloody, for a few more words of advice and counsel. Then into the ring again, all on his own. Does this depict your relationship with God?

Either of these two misconceptions can be deadly, leaving us fragile and weak. We face life, and even God-called ministry, crippled and impaired—if not debilitated.

But the truth is, God is present in both our work and our rest. Even when our rest is recreational, He is there. Psalm 23 speaks of rest, but at the lake? In the meadow? On vacation? Of course! His promise is wherever He leads, wherever we go, He is there. Imagine God saying to you personally, "No matter what you do, no matter where you go, I'm with you. In your work, but not only in your work. In your rest, but not only in your rest. I'm here, out there, everywhere. That's all there is to it. Here, and here to stay."

When we answer God's call to quiet, He refreshes us with His love, rejuvenates us with His touch, and reminds us with His grace that by His mercy He will strengthen us in our work. That we are always in His sight, never away from His thoughts, and covered by His hand. That whatever touches us, touches Him. And, just as He calls us to work and responsibility, He also calls us to rest. Just as He promised Moses, He promises you and me: "My Presence will go with you, and I will give you rest."

———

Consider these words of wisdom:

116

Come to me, all you who are weary and burdened, and I will give you rest. Take my yoke upon you and learn from me, for I am gentle and humble in heart, and you will find rest for your souls. For my yoke is easy and my burden is light.

—Jesus (Matthew 11:28–30)

Enjoy these words of beauty:

The Lord is my Shepherd, I shall not want,
He maketh me down to lie
In pastures green He leadeth me
The quiet waters by.

My soul crieth out: "Restore me again,
And give me the strength to take
The narrow path of righteousness,
E'en for Thine own name's sake."

Yea, though I should walk the valley of death,
Yet what should I fear from ill?
For Thou art with me, and Thy rod
And staff support me still.

His yoke is easy, His burden is light;
I've found it so, I've found it so;
He leadeth me by day and by night,
Where living waters flow.

—R. E. Hudson
(from *Melodies of Praise*,
GPH 1957)

———————

Do you ever live as if your spiritual life is, or depends on, your work, duty, or ministry? Comment.

Do you ever live as if your spiritual life were separate from your work, duty, or ministry? Comment.

117

In a written prayer, make a new commitment to reconnect all three: your work, your rest, and your day-to-day walk with Christ.

Chapter · 18 ·

Reflections

Read Psalm 116:1–7.
Reflect on these words from verse 7:

> *Be at rest once more, O my soul, for the* LORD *has been good to you.*

Once more, the psalmist says, *I've been at rest before. . . .* as if rest isn't something you come to at the end, but rather frequently along the way. And for very good reason: rest gives time for reflection, for remembering. Reflective rest provides time and place to visit certain reminders, time to recall the past and its lessons. But even more, it provides time and place to recall God's goodness, provision, and love. Reflective rest gives opportunity to access our reference points—remembering what He did then, what He can do now, what He will do in the future. Did you notice all the references to the past in our reading for today? Look at the passage again.

As painful as the past can sometimes be to think about, reflection is often the best way to realize that it is only by God's mercy that some of us survived at all. To remind ourselves of circumstances that could have finished us off but didn't. To remind ourselves that God in His mercy saw us through, brought us out, and lifted us up. Reflective rest helps us spend time getting a new perspective on what faces us in the present and future *because of our past*.

Furthermore, reflective rest gives time to think through our decisions, rethink hasty ones, and evaluate where we go from here. Reflective rest gives us the strength to look ahead from the perspective of God's involvement in our past and, with the strength gathered from yesterday, to face today and hope for tomorrow.

When I look over the pathway of my past, marked with my own footprints, crusted over with tears of remorse for my failures, mixed with tears of joy for my successes, I can only say with deep, heartfelt gratitude, "After all I've been through, I'd be a fool not to trust Him. After where I've been, in moments of defeat and triumph, and considering what He's done for me, in me, and even through me, how could I ever doubt He'll continue?"

Do you think God has forgotten you? Have your pain and struggles counted for nothing? Think again. Reflect on God's grace shown to you in the past. Recall His mercy toward you. Whether you are living in difficulty at this moment or not, take strength from your past, no matter how ugly and painful it may be. Remind yourself in reflective rest that the very fact you are where you are today is because you are a trophy of God's grace. Oh, you may need a little polishing, and even some cleaning up, but you are priceless to God—an absolute treasure. If you spend time in reflective rest, He'll tell you himself. It's all part of His call to quiet. Aren't you glad you answered?

Consider these words of wisdom:

> Whatever is true, whatever is noble, whatever is right, whatever is pure, whatever is lovely, whatever is admirable—if anything is excellent or praiseworthy—think about such things.

> —The Apostle Paul, in his letter
> to the Philippians (4:8)

Enjoy these words of beauty:

A wonderful Savior is Jesus, my Lord,
A wonderful Savior to me;

120

He hideth my soul in the cleft of the rock
Where rivers of pleasure I see.

Wonderful Savior is Jesus, my Lord,
He taketh my burden away;
He holdeth me up, and I shall not be moved;
He giveth me strength as my day.

With numberless blessings each moment He crowns,
And, filled with His fullness divine,
I sing in my rapture, oh, glory to God
For such a Redeemer as mine!

He hideth my soul in the cleft of the rock
That shadows a dry, thirsty land;
He hideth my soul in the depths of His love,
And covers me there with His hand,
And covers me there with His hand.

—Fanny J. Crosby

———

Many people take extreme measures and make great effort to forget their past. Why do you suppose that is true?

If you are reading this book and participating in the thought-provoking questions, it is probably true that God has allowed you to come through some trials. How can you look back and see His working in your past?

How does reflective rest help you see God's protective hand in your past?

How does reflecting on God's faithfulness to you in the past help you have faith for His care in the future?

Reflecting on your past, what is one important milestone or turning point that has God's fingerprints on it?

Considering where you've been, and what you're going through at the moment, write a prayer that comes from taking reflective rest:

Chapter
· 19 ·

Rest and
Redirection

Read Psalm 119:57–60.
Reflect on these words from Isaiah 28:12:

"This is the resting place, let the weary rest"; and, "This is the place of repose."

Repent. We're all familiar with the word—the main theme of the evangelist, the heartbeat of the soul winner. The very word that brought us hope as we sought God for personal salvation and relationship with Him. It's a word that we think usually applies to a sinner once, but it is also a promise for a grace-saved sinner, like me. Repentance speaks of the kindness of God and the time He gives me by withholding His judgment so that I might see the error of my ways, make a decision to commit myself to His way, and go on from there. And the moments of rest I take in His presence give me the opportunity to do just that.

How about you? Do you ever get so sick of yourself that you prefer to keep busy rather than have time alone—to think? Me too. After all, we reason, I'm the last person I'd want to be with right now. Why should God want to be with me? And all the while we sense His beckoning: "Come close. . . . Rest."

This is when it is most important to realize that rest for the sake of repentance is critically needed.

Are you like me and get so busy that you slip into the

old habit of taking things into your own hands? Often with results that are far less than desired but exactly what one might expect? Trying too hard to make things work? Holding so tight for control that all the joy is lost? If so, it's time for a rest stop for repentance.

How long has it been since what you accomplished had more of God's fingerprints on it than your own? Want to have a fresh touch of God on your heart and evidence of His touch in your life? Yeah, I know—me too. Then these "rests of repentance" are just what we both need.

These are the recesses from the rush of life that give us opportunity not only to reflect on issues, relationships, and goals, but the time necessary to make a renewed commitment to a faith and way of life that involves turning from a previous, or even present, way of living. A new way, a new decision, and a renewed faith are the fruitful results of repentant rest.

These momentary reflective rests can actually be life-changing. A change of mind and attitude through repentance can change the entire course of your life through a simple, even small, God-directed correction. It is a faith-filled moment when we can take a deep breath of God's forgiveness and exhale old, stale, selfish motives and self-centered ambition. When we can once again refresh ourselves in the faithful love of our heavenly Father. Once more sense the cleansing of the blood of Christ shed for our sins and be infused by the strength of the Holy Spirit, who graces us with the strength and desire to do things God's way. It's when we realize that we can carry out our decision to turn from our old ways and commit ourselves to God's way.

And it can happen in a brief moment of rest. What are we waiting for, why do we delay? Why struggle any longer? Won't you join me in a moment of refreshing rest and repentance?

"This," the Word of God says, "is the place of repose." Repentance and rest—often the result of answering God's call to quiet.

———

Consider these words of wisdom:

When, in the course of a day's engagements, our conscience witnesses against us that we have sinned, we should at once confess our guilt, claim by faith the cleansing of the blood of Christ, and so wash our hands in innocence.

—David M'Intyre,
Hidden Life of Prayer

Enjoy these words of beauty:

My hope of salvation is steadfast and sure,
I've builded my house on foundation secure,
The rock of His Word that shall ever endure,
The promise unfailing is mine.

The tempter may strive to ensnare and defeat,
And many a pitfall is laid for my feet,
But grace all availing, each trial shall meet,
The promise unfailing is mine.

How happy my lot since the Lord has control,
What glad, sweet assurance abides in my soul;
My heart sings with joy as I press towards the goal,
The promise unfailing is mine.

—Haldor Lillenas

When was the last time the Lord spoke to you concerning your flaws and faults, gently and with great kindness leading you to repentance?

When was the last time a sour situation surfaced and you repented rather than defended yourself? With what result? Please comment.

125

When, if ever, did you last feel totally released from guilt, completely innocent?

How do the words of 1 John 1:9 apply to you and give you hope?

Why is the statement "Of course it's my fault, it's always my fault" personally defeating and conflicting with true repentance?

If you were to stop right now and give God the freedom to search your heart, what do you think He'd bring up that you might need to repent of?

Write your prayer here:

Chapter • 20 •

Rested and Restored

Read Psalm 25.
Reflect on these words from Psalm 23:3:

He restores my soul.

Reaping the consequences of sin and open to attack by opportunistic enemies, David repeats the truth that his only hope is in God and God alone. Once again he learns the lesson that he can't trust in himself. His judgment has proven to be faulty, his strength has failed, and he finally acknowledges his only recourse is to turn to God. To depend on His mercy, grace, love, uprightness, and faithfulness, especially when David knows that in himself he possesses none of those things. Scholars tell us that the prayer of Psalm 25 may have been after the author had sinned willfully—gotten himself into a pack of trouble at his own dishonest hand. Wow! I can identify!

Yet the writer of this beautiful prayer of contrition knew that at the end of himself and all his failures, God was waiting, ready to hear and answer his prayers. "I've totally blown it, God," he seems to convey. "Once again, I must confess my only hope is in you. Goodness knows, I've made a complete mess of things and proven to be an idiot once again."

Such honesty, such open admission of wrongdoing! If I were to be completely honest, I'd have to admit that at such times in my own life I tend to *fudge* a little and, with a whine, approach the situation as a victim, certainly not the perpetrator. Well, at first anyway. But it doesn't work. If I am to understand the full meaning of restoration, I must quickly admit my own fault. Then, and only then, can I declare my only hope is in God and in His intervention.

Perhaps you have discovered the same.

What patience God has with us! Over and over again we must come to Him for restoration. Many times our lives are scarred with our mistakes, our relationships strained by our carelessness and selfishness. Sometimes our paths are strewed with obstacles of our own making, leaving our souls in need of repair and restoration.

I can't help but think of two guys on TV who repair and restore furniture. I've noticed that repair has to precede refinishing, and beautiful restoration is the result. It reminds me of our lives and our coming to God again and again. Many of us just want the refinishing and restoration without the needed repair. We wait until our lives are falling apart and headed for certain disastrous ruin before we take the time to go to our Father for help.

However, we can learn to avoid the need for such extensive repair if we will simply, through our moments of rest, refreshing, reflection, and repentance, keep up a maintenance program of restoration. Ask the guys on TV: isn't it easier to repair a scratch or small dent than to work on a piece of furniture so neglected it borders on a total loss? Of course it is. A little scratch remover, a good polish, and there you are! It's the same with us.

By making room in our regular schedule for moments with the Master, including not only worship and devotion but also rest, it is possible to go on for years without need for major repair. A little restoration now and then keeps us up to speed with God's will for our lives, our souls healthy and intact.

It's like getting a periodic make-over. Bringing your spiritual self up-to-date. Keeping current with what God is doing in and through you. Keeping you prepared for facing daily life with your best foot forward. Your finest traits polished and submitted to God for His use. Your strengths kept pure for His commission. Your talents yielded for His purpose.

These times of ongoing restoration in His presence aren't only for your benefit, but that He be glorified in you. Not to give you a better image, but that His perfect image be always apparent in you. Isn't that what you really want?

———

Consider these words of wisdom:

> Jesus Christ came meaning for us to be restored to the state from which we had fallen. Salvation, then, is the state in which the whole inner man—the heart, the will, the life—is given up to the glory and service of God. . . . The enthusiastic devotion of the complete inner man is what is asked of us. . . .

—Andrew Murray,
*The Believer's Secret
of a Perfect Heart*
(taken from *Mighty Is Your Hand*,
edited by David Hazard)

Enjoy these words of beauty:

> I am Thine, O Lord—I have heard Thy voice,
> And it told Thy love to me;
> But I long to rise in the arms of faith
> And be closer drawn to Thee.
>
> Consecrate me now to Thy service, Lord,
> By the pow'r of grace divine;
> Let my soul look up with a steadfast hope
> And my will be lost in Thine.
>
> O the pure delight of a single hour
> That before Thy throne I spend,
> When I kneel in pray'r and with Thee, my God,
> I commune as friend with friend.
>
> Draw me nearer, nearer, blessed Lord,
> To the cross where Thou hast died;
> Draw me nearer, nearer, nearer, blessed Lord,
> To Thy precious, bleeding side.

—Fanny J. Crosby

_____

What do you think would change in you if you seriously asked God to examine your heart and life and bring His redemptive, refinishing touch to any area He chose?

Where do you think He would begin?

Are you willing to let Him restore you there? Comment:

How has this section on rest changed your previous definition of the word?

How have these concepts changed your usual quiet time practices or habits?

At this point, what does "answering God's call to quiet" mean to you?

How is that different than when you first began this study?

Do you have further thoughts and prayers? Write them here:

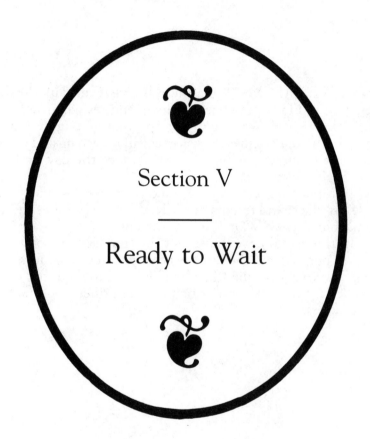

Section V

———

Ready to Wait

HERE WE ARE. We've come away, we've reveled in silence, reveried in God's presence and love, and rested, answering His call to quiet. We've gotten a spiritual tune-up, warmed up our religious engines. Now we feel all revved up and ready to go. It's time to get right out there, face the day, and do life. Right? Wrong.

In Mark 6:31 Jesus says, "Come ye yourselves apart into a desert place, and rest a while" (KJV). A *while*. Linger here, don't hurry away. Wait. Tarry. Hang out.

In this section, we'll discover the true meaning of waiting: its purpose and the skills necessary to obey God in waiting. There's lots of life to be lived for and in God, but first, let's learn this important principle. The principle of *waiting in readiness*.

Chapter
• 21 •

Linger a Little Longer

Read John 15:1–11.
Reflect on these words from verse 9:

"Now remain in my love."

"Here's your hat, what's your hurry?" This funny old joke between friends speaks quite accurately of the hurried pace of our day. Almost everyone I know jumps out of bed with their feet running.

Family members hurry past each other in the mad dash to be first in the bathroom. After a quick turn in the shower, they leap into their clothes, bolt down instant breakfasts, or skip eating altogether and race out the door. The modern mother deposits her children at their various destinations before she goes to her job or place of volunteer work for the day. All this before 9:00 A.M.!

Her evening isn't much different. Picking up the children and transporting them to their after-school activities, she manages to squeeze her household errands between sports, piano lessons, and dance rehearsals. Finally, she heads for home to an evening of supervising homework, library visits, church activities, community involvement, cooking, cleaning, and laundry. Exhausted, she falls into bed, only to begin the same race again the next day.

We often shake our heads in dismay at our packed schedules and appointment books. There's hardly a moment left to breathe, much less rest or relax. And lest you think it's only mothers who are under such pressure to be everywhere at once, think again. It's universal. Women and men from every walk of life, and even our children and teens, are rushing in this hurried pace from one activity to another.

Quiet time? In such a harried, hurried life? Who are we kidding? Grabbing a quick moment of silence before leaving our cars to walk into the workplace is the most quiet time many busy women can manage. In light of our action-packed lives, to suggest that we take an unhurried fifteen minutes, or even half an hour of quietness in the presence of God seems ludicrous, like a faraway fantasy of some unhurried life generations ago. Yet that's not *only* what I'm suggesting. I'm also strongly advising that we not only make the most of those quiet moments, but we stretch them beyond what we think is possible.

"Remain" is not only *my* advice, but the counsel of Scripture. Stay, linger, wait, the Bible says. Slow down, let your life idle for a moment longer than you had planned. Purposely, decisively, come to a standstill and give that time to waiting in God's love.

If you have made it this far in this book, you may already feel you have done the impossible by creating space and making place for quiet in your life. Aren't you glad you have overcome the difficulties and have begun to respond to God's call to quiet, even for short intervals? Yet, isn't there more?

Look at it this way: though you have taken the time, have you spent these minutes in quiet with an unhurried heart? Have precious moments been rushed with the pressures and responsibilities awaiting you? Have you given this time to God? Perhaps you have participated in this study out of a sense of duty or self-discipline. If so, you have missed the blessing of this message and its application for your relationship with God.

We may be able to tend to the ever-increasing demands of our lives by moving faster, trying harder, and becoming more efficient in time-management, but we can't tend to our relationship with God that way. The love of our Savior and the sacrifice He made on our behalf deserves our unhurried, undivided attention. When we stop to think about it, we realize it's the pace of our life that usurps our devotional time and energy—certainly not our loving Lord.

If you see the need for spending a little more time exclusively in His presence, try this: after your quiet time today, close your Bible, this book, and your appointment book as well, and lean your head back against your chair. Breathe deeply and relax. Determine to take two more minutes, that's all, 120 seconds of uninterrupted time in God's presence. Just you and God—alone, for just a little longer. Set a timer if you must, but determine to give those two minutes completely to Him.

What major upset or calamity will invade your life because you took two minutes to do nothing but sit in quiet reverie with the King of Kings and Lord of Lords? In response to the question "Here's your hat, what's your hurry?" say, "Put down the hat, I'm in no hurry—no hurry at all."

Consider these words of wisdom:

> Would God that we might get some right conception of what the influence would be on a life spent, not in thought, or imagination, or effort, but in the power of the Holy Spirit, wholly waiting on God.
>
> —Andrew Murray,
> *Waiting on God*

Enjoy these words of beauty:

> Great God! Attend while Zion sings
> The joy that from Thy presence springs:
> To spend one day with Thee on earth
> Exceeds a thousand days of mirth.
>
> Might I enjoy the meanest place
> Within Thy house, O God of grace,
> Not tents of ease, nor thrones of power,
> Should tempt my feet to leave Thy door.
>
> —Isaac Watts

After spending two or more additional minutes waiting in God's presence, ask yourself the following:

Did I spend these minutes unhurried, or did my heart still strain to get back to "life as usual"?

What are some practical ways I can take the hurry out of my life?

How can I take it out of my heart?

If God were to give me back those few minutes later in the day, where in my schedule would He most likely take them from?

Chapter · 22 ·

Open Your Heart

Read Psalm 37:3–9.
Reflect on these words from Nahum 1:7:

He cares for those who trust in him.

How much do you trust God? Look into the face of your child. Do you trust God as much as that child trusts you?

Andrew Murray, in his book *Waiting on God*, says that the mind gathers knowledge from God's Word and prepares it as food by which the heart, along with the inner life, is to be nourished. He goes on to warn us of the terrible danger of leaning on our own understanding, in other words, of depending on the mind alone or depending only on our mental apprehension of divine things. It isn't enough that we apprehend or even mentally appreciate the truth, but that we live it. That happens in the heart.

In contemporary society we are in danger of being so rushed and pressured that we don't have time for much more than reading a few verses of God's Word at one sitting. It is almost unthinkable to take additional time to absorb it yet deeper within ourselves—to allow the personal meaning of God's precious promises to reach our hearts.

Yet even in the middle of our busiest, noisiest lives and schedules God still calls us to quietness—to wait before Him, His Word in our minds, His love in our hearts, until we know more than the application, but also experience the *implica-*

tion of His presence in our lives.

To answer His call to quiet, we now include such words as continue, abide, stay, wait, tarry, or linger in our devotional understanding. There is more to being with God than prayer, praise, and even worship. There are times when it is not only appropriate but essential to our relationship with Him that we extend our time—in silence—together with Him. Wordlessly giving Him unreserved accessibility to a heart opened and unhurried in His presence. Putting our demanding lives on hold while we purposely dwell in His love awhile longer. Postponing our daily schedule, setting aside an evening or even a weekend, simply to walk or sit or rest, putting all our attention and devotion on Him. Letting Him look deep within our open heart, searching us with His mercy, loving us because of His grace.

And to do so, we must trust Him at the same level a toddler trustingly clings to his mother. We must trust Him to hear our prayers, receive our praise, but even more believe that He will be true to His Word and care for us in response to that trust.

Take a little extra time to trust Him today. Nothing more. No words, no prayers or praise—simply an open heart, choosing to wait in His presence until the assurance comes that He has accepted what no one can offer in our behalf— our complete trust.

———

Consider these words of wisdom:

> What He asks of us in the way of surrender and obedience and desire and trust is all comprised in one word: *waiting* on Him, waiting for His salvation.

—Andrew Murray,
Waiting on God

Enjoy these words of beauty:

Simply trusting every day,
Trusting through a stormy way;
Even when my faith is small,
Trusting Jesus, that is all.

140

Brightly doth His Spirit shine
Into this poor heart of mine;
While He leads I cannot fall;
Trusting Jesus, that is all.

Singing if my way is clear;
Praying if the path be drear;
If in danger, for Him call;
Trusting Jesus, that is all.

Trusting Him while life shall last,
Trusting Him till earth be past;
Till within the jasper wall:
Trusting Jesus, that is all.

Trusting as the moments fly,
Trusting as the days go by;
Trusting Him whate'er befall,
Trusting Jesus, that is all.

—Edgar Page Stites

———

How can you measure your trust in God?

How do your past experiences affect your level of trust in God?

How do your past experiences of trusting God affect your future?

141

What is there in your life at the present time that is requiring you to trust God at a level that may be a bit uncomfortable for you?

How can you exercise your trust muscles more?

Chapter
· 23 ·

Waiting With a Listening Heart

Read Isaiah 50:4–5.
Reflect on these words from John 10:4:

His sheep follow him because they know his voice.

"Yeah, I know." What parent of a teen hasn't heard those words? You talk and explain in detail, hoping to get through, and the response is "Yeah, I know." But later, the story is quite different.

"What do you mean I can't go to the game?"

"You didn't say I had to clean my room *before* the party!"

And our reply? "You didn't listen, did you?"

Typical adolescent hearing loss. I hate to admit it, but I have to confess I've done the same thing in my quiet times. Offering my heart, but closing my ears.

"I want to be completely yours. . . . Yes, Lord, look at my heart. . . . See, it is all yours." I've prayed this prayer more than once during the four decades I've served the Lord. "My heart, my life, my possessions—they're all yours."

All . . . but with the exception that I haven't always given Him my full attention or listened to His voice as He spoke to my heart.

"Oh, c'mon," some of you may say, "do you expect me to believe God actually speaks to us?"

Yes, exactly. But you see, it's more than a belief that He could or someday will—it is based on His Word that He *does*.

"My sheep," He says, "know my voice. My sheep listen."

When we extend our devotional times to include drawn-out moments of openhearted silence, let us also listen. Listen for the voice of the Shepherd speaking words of love and encouragement. Giving instruction and wisdom. Whispering His thoughts about us into our hearts, giving us hope, and filling us with faith. New ideas are born while listening to the voice of God. Doors of ministry are opened, confusion is cleared, and insight is given. Difficulties are put into proper perspective when we listen with our hearts for God's voice. God's purposes are revealed and established within us as we listen in silence. Waiting in quiet listening, we hear anew His call on our lives. We learn when to say yes to God's will and are given the courage to say no to temptation and distractions.

Furthermore, when we learn to listen in quietness and recognize the voice of the Shepherd, we are no longer fooled by the voice of a stranger. Accusations against our worth and value fall fruitless without damaging us. Attacks against our integrity and purpose sound shallow and false. Whispers of gossip about past shameful secrets have no harmful effects because we know them to come from the voice of the stranger. Mocking remarks about our failures fail to discourage us because all the while the stranger's voice reeks with destruction and devastation, the voice of the Shepherd continues with love and healing, worth and hope, forgiveness and restoration.

How long has it been since you heard the voice of the kindhearted Shepherd (Jesus) speak lovingly into your heart and touch the depths of your soul? How long since you took the time to silence other voices coming at you from every direction and simply remained still and listened for His voice?

Consider these words of wisdom:

In waiting on God, the first thought is of *the God upon whom we wait*. We enter His presence, and feel we need just to be quiet, so that He, as God, can overshadow us with Himself. God longs to reveal Himself, to fill us with Himself.

And when you are praying, let there be intervals of silence, reverent stillness of soul, in which you yield yourself to God, in case He may have [something] He wishes to teach you or to work in you.

—Andrew Murray,
Waiting on God

Enjoy these words of beauty:

Sing them over again to me,
　　Wonderful words of life!
Let me more of their beauty see,
　　Wonderful words of life!
Words of life and beauty,
　　Teach me faith and duty!
Beautiful words! Wonderful words!
　　Wonderful words of life!
Beautiful words! Wonderful words!
　　Wonderful words of life!

Christ, the blessed One, gives to all
　　Wonderful words of life!
Sinner, list to the loving call,
　　Wonderful words of life!
All so freely given,
　　Wooing us to heaven!
Beautiful words! Wonderful words!
　　Wonderful words of life!
Beautiful words! Wonderful words!
　　Wonderful words of life!

Sweetly echo the gospel call,
　　Wonderful words of life!
Offer pardon and peace to all,
　　Wonderful words of life!
Jesus, only Saviour,
　　Sanctify forever!
Beautiful words! Wonderful words!
　　Wonderful words of life!
Beautiful words! Wonderful words!
　　Wonderful words of life!

—Philip P. Bliss

145

———————

Are you ready to *listen* to God, to take the time and make the necessary silence to hear Him?

How have you heard Him speak to you in the past?

If you hesitate to wait in silence, listening for and then to Him, do you know why?

When you listen, are you afraid He might not speak, or are you afraid of what He might say? Why?

If God were to say something to you He's wanted to say for a long time, what do you think that would be?

Write here a prayer of commitment to listen:

Chapter
· 24 ·

Listening
With an
"Open-
minded" Heart

Read Isaiah 43:18–21.
Reflect on these words from Isaiah 48:6:

"From now on I will tell you of new things."

Nothing triggers resistance in the heart of the established and traditional Christian as much as the mention of *change*. "Do what?" we protest. "But we've always done it this way!"

Yet change is what the Christian life is all about. From the very beginning of our walk with Christ, we are called to change.

"Come follow me," Jesus invited His first disciples, "and I will make you . . ." Changed from fishers of fish to fishers of men.

Paul wrote in his second letter to the Corinthians these words: "Therefore, if anyone is in Christ, he is a new creation; the old has gone, the new has come!" (5:17). Change—normal for the Christian life.

When we take extended time to wait upon God, open-hearted and listening, we can expect new things to result. New ideas, new vision, renewed strength—all are part of encountering God in moments of silent devotional reverie. Just being with Him in this manner will bring many into a new place with God. A new intimacy, a new depth of relationship, and a wonderful new awareness of His closeness and care. The sweetness of His presence is awakened in our souls as we give place to Him in quietness.

So let us enter His presence, in quietness and solitude. Then let us linger a little longer. Waiting for God, waiting on God. And then, with expectation, not only open our hearts to give love to Him, but also to receive from Him.

Let us be open to the suggestions the Holy Spirit would whisper into our minds and hearts. Let us listen for His voice in such a way that we are receptive to His word, that we are amenable to His will, and readily available to His working within our hearts.

Who knows but that the insight to your problem lies just ahead in that moment of silence, waiting in renewed submission to His presence? Perhaps the direction you seek is waiting for you as you wait on Him. Could the healing you've been seeking come gently, without fanfare, in this quietness before your loving Lord? Anything is possible in such sweet, unhurried, intimate fellowship with Jesus.

It is possible that some of you reading this book have never before known Christ at this dimension. If you are one of these, let me encourage you to slow down your life, make room for silence and solitude before your King, then wait just a little longer in His presence. There is a relationship with your heavenly Father like nothing you've ever known before. He longs to be gracious to His children. Unfortunately, many never take the time necessary to experience such grace. Will you?

Will you find the time and the courage to put your busy life on hold for fifteen minutes, maybe even thirty? I promise you—but even more than that, God promises you—there are new things ahead. Things you cannot even imagine. Things so wonderful that no matter what happens in your life, no matter what pain you have encountered or where you have failed, He has new things to tell you. All you have to do is come to Him with an open, listening heart.

God is calling—calling you to quiet. Will you answer?

Consider these words of wisdom:

150

Learn to say of every want, and every failure, and every lack of needful grace: I have waited too little upon God, or He would have given me in due season all I needed. And say then too—My *soul, wait thou only upon God!*

—Andrew Murray,
Waiting on God

Enjoy these words of beauty:

Break Thou the bread of life, Dear Lord, to me,
As Thou didst break the loaves beside the sea;
Beyond the sacred page I seek Thee, Lord;
My spirit pants for Thee, O living Word!

Bless Thou the truth, dear Lord, to me, to me,
As Thou didst bless the bread by Galilee;
Then shall all bondage cease, all fetters fall,
And I shall find my peace, my all in all.

Teach me to live, dear Lord, only for Thee,
As Thy disciples lived in Galilee;
Then, all my struggles o'er, the vict'ry won,
I shall behold Thee, Lord, the living One.

—Mary Ann Lathbury

Are you by nature a skeptic? An explorer? A risk-taker? A "play-it-safe" conservative? Other?

Have you ever had your hands slapped for being too excited about spiritual things? Comment:

151

Have you learned to keep secrets? Could God share His confidences with you? Comment:

How do all of the previous help or hinder your coming to God with an "openminded" heart?

If God were to tell you an absolutely new truth about yourself and your relationship with Him, what would be the most outlandish thing He could possibly say?

Is there any possibility that there is truth in what you wrote above? Why or why not?

What further thoughts are you having about being in God's presence in the manner presented in this section of the book?

Chapter
· 25 ·

Ready and
Waiting

Read Luke 12:35–40.
Then reflect on these verses:

Remind the people . . . to be ready to do whatever is good. . . . Titus 3:1

Be prepared to give an answer to everyone who asks you to give the reason for the hope that you have. 1 Peter 3:15

. . . willing . . . eager to serve . . . 1 Peter 5:2

Preparedness. A word we hear a lot living in California. Ready to swing into action at any moment. But more than being prepared for natural disasters such as earthquakes, tornadoes, or wild fires, the Bible teaches us to live in a state of continual readiness. That's right, prepared and equipped to act or be used with less than a moment's notice.

As believers, we are to live in prepared expectancy that the return of Jesus Christ could occur at any moment. It is the one thing that gives us hope when we observe the world around us decaying and sin running unchecked in global proportions.

We do, however, find another call to readiness in the Bible: to be constantly on the alert for ways in which God can use us while we wait for the return of His Son. Wide awake, ever watchful. Ready to fill a need, to touch a wounded heart, or to pray for a person in crisis. But even

153

more, ready to move at His command, yield to His control, and answer His call on our lives and our time. In other words, ready and waiting.

. . . be ready to do . . .

You never know when you'll be called on, when at the end of quietly waiting in silence and solitude for Him, He will speak to you about "kingdom" business. It is critical that we learn to wait in readiness: vigilant, watchful, and attentive, yes—and more. Ready, but restrained as well.

It's hard, this waiting in readiness. So many needs, so many hurts right around us—among our friends and in our families, among our co-workers and in our churches. However, if we haven't learned to wait in readiness, we run the risk of moving ahead of God. Moving in on His work, instead of moving *in* His will. Whenever God is answering a prayer, even when He's bringing that answer through us, He has been working on both ends of the need—in the heart of the recipient as well as in the answer-bringer. If the full work isn't done at both ends, the connection fails and the answer can be delayed.

We see a need; we have the resources to meet that need. We belong to God; our resources belong to Him as well. What's mine is His and at His disposal. So far so good. But when we step out without waiting for His timing, His command, and His urging, what might have been an answer to another's need and prayer could be delivered prematurely, and the person receiving the answer may have to learn a lesson of faith and patience all over again.

The Word is clear: be *ready* to do. It is not just *do*. Ready and available, not to the need but to God. If you see a person in need, it is God's business. It only becomes your business when He makes it your business. People who wait in readiness are most often included in such matters.

Be prepared to give an answer to everyone who asks you . . .

We all know them; they are the ones who give their opinion, their biblical insight, and their "word from God" indiscriminately. Pushing their way into most situations they encounter, they rarely, if ever, wait to be asked. They are continually ready, but haven't learned the powerful dynamic of waiting in that readiness.

154

Even in witnessing to the unsaved, we must be watchful, waiting, and prepared to speak when the opportunity arises. But remember, God is working on both ends, preparing the message-bearer and the receiver at the same time.

When you have taken all the necessary steps to become a quiet listener, a waiter on God, His nudges become altogether more clearly felt and understood. Witnessing opportunities present themselves through the sincere hearts of the seekers, the hungry after God. Am I suggesting that we never take the initiative in evangelism? Of course not, but I am suggesting that we need to listen closely and make sure it *is* God who is compelling us to speak. That we are waiting in readiness to speak when God urges from within. After all, He knows where the ready hearts are. The waiting and ready worker is led to a ripe and waiting harvest.

. . . *willing* . . . *eager to serve* . . .

Willing, eager, not pushy, not forceful. Once again, remember, God is working where? Right! At both ends of the prayer. Doesn't it make sense that if He is able to make you willing, to do a work of eagerness and preparedness within you, He is also preparing a place for such service to happen? How often have we forged ahead in our eagerness and either made a complete mess of things or settled for less than what God would have offered had we waited in readiness?

It can be frustrating to wait in readiness. Yet while we wait, let us yield to God even more, for even a greater depth of work to occur in our hearts, motives, and maturity so that when the door of opportunity opens and He beckons us to enter, we are even more prepared for effective service than ever before.

Ready and waiting. The mark of a submitted heart. The hangtag on the listening heart. The advantage of the open-minded heart. The hallmark of a Christ-follower.

Okay, are you on your toes? Are all systems go? Do you sense you are on the verge of something great in God? On the brink of new spiritual depth or Christian service? Are you living as if on call, handy and accessible to God without delay? Good. Then wait right there. He'll let you know when it's time to go, do, or speak.

155

Consider these words of wisdom:

> The waiting is to teach us our absolute dependence upon God's mighty working, and to make us in perfect patience place ourselves at His disposal.

—Andrew Murray,
Waiting on God

Enjoy these words of beauty:

Ready to go, ready to stay,
Ready my place to fill;
Ready for service, lowly or great,
Ready to do His will.

Ready to suffer grief or pain,
Ready to stand the test;
Ready to stay at home and send
Others if He sees best.

Ready to go, ready to bear,
Ready to watch and pray;
Ready to stand aside and give,
Till He shall clear the way.

Ready to speak, ready to think,
Ready with heart and brain;
Ready to stand where He sees fit,
Ready to bear the strain.

Ready to speak, ready to warn,
Ready o'er souls to yearn;
Ready in life, ready in death,
Ready for His return.

Ready to go, ready to stay,
Ready my place to fill;
Ready for service, lowly or great,
Ready to do His will.

—A. C. Palmer

Are you more apt to see a need and fill it or wait for God's direction?

Do you ever run ahead of God's timing and will? Recall a specific instance, if possible.

Are you willing to be ready and waiting, even if it's frustrating sometimes?

Are you willing to be ready and waiting to move in God's will on demand, even if it means personal sacrifice or inconvenience?

Write your commitment to be ready and waiting in a prayer:

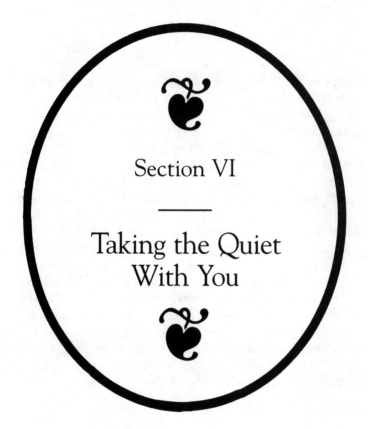

Section VI

—

Taking the Quiet
With You

"I CAN'T STAY HERE all day," I reluctantly admitted. "As wonderful as this is, I have to get to work."

So what do we do when we have to reenter life with its demands and pressures? We take the quiet with us. It's as simple as that. The presence of God isn't relegated to your devotional time or quiet place; He is available to us at every moment in every circumstance. We return to our quiet places frequently, of course, but more than that, we take the strength received during these times right back into the mainstream of family, friends, work, and schedules.

We do what Brother Lawrence called *practicing the presence of God.*

In the next five devotional studies, we will review the principles learned in this book when you took the step to answer God's call to quiet. Then we'll look at how we can apply those principles to daily life. By the end of this book, you will not only have answered your heavenly Father's call to quiet but you will also know how to let that quietness touch and affect the rest of your life.

Chapter
· 26 ·

Come Away—
Stay Away

Review Section I.
Read 2 Corinthians 6:14—7:1.
Reflect on these words from Leviticus 15:31:

> *"You must keep the Israelites separate from things that make them unclean, so they will not die in their uncleanness for defiling my dwelling place, which is among them."*

And on these words from Isaiah 52:11:

> *Depart, depart, go out from there! Touch no unclean thing! Come out from it and be pure, you who carry the vessels of the LORD.*

It is definitely hard to leave our precious hiding place of refuge and strength, where we quietly bask in the presence of the Lord. But the rest of life is waiting; there is work to be done, appointments to keep. How tempting it is to lean toward separatism—to withdraw from life and its pressures, to say nothing of its filth.

Yet, realistically, we know we can't stay in our refuge forever. We *can*, however, live by the same call to come away, maintaining our quietness throughout our busiest day.

The Bible portrays God's people as a most unusual group. The Old Testament tells us they had many unusual religious and lifestyle practices—all for one purpose: to be known among themselves and to others as different, as God's people.

They were held to a higher call of obedience than their pagan neighbors, summoned to a higher standard than everyone else. Although the details of the Hebrew law are no longer required of New Covenant Christians, the higher call to obedience and godly living, which are the basis of that law, still stand.

It's not easy living and working among nonbelievers. Yet that's exactly what we're called to do. And while we're called to be with them, we are not to be like them. We are to love, serve, work alongside the unredeemed of our culture, but at the same time be so different in our moral standards, our integrity, and dependability that we stand out as unique. We are sent out of our safe *Christian* environment in order to bring the influence of our Lord and Savior where it's needed the most—to a lost and dying world.

It's not easy being *in* but not *of* the world. But it helps to keep our eyes focused on the purpose for our being out there. How many Christians do you know who resist being anywhere other than a Christian environment? Some prefer to patronize only *Christian* businesses, others attend only *Christian* schools. People I consider strong Christians refuse to belong to any community organization because these groups aren't *Christian*. But isn't that the reason we *should* involve ourselves in such groups? Is it right to leave the world around us devoid of our influence and witness? Can we point the way to Christ if we have no association with sinners?

Let us maintain our sense of God's quietness within our souls by accepting His call to go out, sent as it were as sheep among wolves. Maintaining our uniqueness, not letting the world pressure us into relaxing our standards; staying away from unholy alliances, certainly, but standing near enough to God to hear His quiet call to touch those around us, to bring healing and hope through Jesus Christ wherever possible.

We don't *come away* to be with God as His child, and then go out into our daily lives and carry out our responsibilities as though we didn't belong to Him. Rather, we take the precious reassurance of His presence with us. You see, when we learn to answer God's call to quiet, eventually we will hear Him call us to other places as well.

Consider these words of wisdom:

> The time of business is no different from the time of prayer. In the noise and clatter of my kitchen, I possess God as tranquilly as if I were upon my knees before the Blessed Sacrament.
>
> —Brother Lawrence, *Practicing the Presence of God*

Enjoy these words of beauty:

> Take the name of Jesus with you,
> Child of sorrow and of woe;
> It will joy and comfort give you,
> Take it then where'er you go.
>
> Take the name of Jesus ever
> As a shield from every snare;
> If temptations round you gather,
> Breathe that holy name in prayer.
>
> At the name of Jesus bowing,
> Falling prostrate at His feet,
> King of Kings in heaven we'll crown Him,
> When our journey is complete.
>
> Precious Name, oh, how sweet!
> Hope of earth and joy of heaven.
> Precious Name, oh, how sweet!
> Hope of earth and joy of heaven.
>
> —Lydia Baxter

What situations do you face every day that tempt you to conform, rather than be different from those around you?

163

Have you ever been excluded because of your Christian faith? Explain:

Have you ever considered that just being different because you are living for Christ is a way to "come away and stay away" from the world? Comment:

Below, write your prayerful commitment to be different, even when thrown into the mainstream of the world and its decay:

Chapter
· 27 ·

Come
With Me,
Be With Me,
Go With Me

Review Section II
Read Exodus 33:12–15.
Reflect on these words from Matthew 28:20:

"And surely I will be with you always, to the very end of the age."

When God calls us to quiet, His presence can become as warm and comfortable as a close and deep friendship. So when we realize that our quiet time has to come to an end, that we have to get on with our day, it can feel as though we're leaving the company of a dear friend. Yet as we go throughout the day, facing our workplace or volunteer commitments, let us not forget that relating to God goes beyond merely an encouraging and precious friendship. He goes with us, where no one else can. He has promised never to leave us.

You trusted Him enough to be alone with Him, and you can trust Him to go with you as you leave this quiet, sheltered place. All you have to do is take this private intimacy with God, tuck it in your heart, and carry it with you everywhere you go. Carry the knowledge that God is with you no matter what confronts you today.

When the job becomes overwhelming, remember God is with you. When the family is too demanding, take a moment to check back inside and revisit the ever-available presence of God within your heart. When the battle to make ends meet rages out of control, God is there. When sickness threatens to overtake, you know it—He's there. And when you feel as though the whole world is about to crash around you, step back and remember, you're not alone—He will save you.

All it takes is a quick inward glance to get back in touch with the peace and quiet from your time alone with God. A deep breath to refocus on His closeness. A conscious effort to maintain intimacy with Him.

Even though you have to go out from here, you never have to fear being distant or separated from Him. He promises.

Consider these words of wisdom:

> My God, since You are with me, and since it is Your will that I should apply my mind to these outward things, I pray that You will give me the grace to remain with You and keep company with You.
>
> —Brother Lawrence, *Practicing the Presence of God*

Enjoy these words of beauty:

> Father in the morning unto Thee I pray;
> Let Thy loving kindness keep me through the day.
> At the busy noontide, pressed with work and care,
> Then I'll wait with Jesus till He hear my prayer.
>
> When the evening shadows chase away the light,
> Father, then I'll pray Thee, bless Thy child tonight.
> Thus in life's glad morning, in its bright noonday,
> In its shadowy evening, ever will I pray.
>
> I will pray, I will pray, ever will I pray;
> Morning, noon, and evening, unto Thee I'll pray.
>
> —Author Unknown

When do you need to be aware of God's presence more than any other time of the day?

How can you return to the inner place of being alone with Him during that time?

How can you remember to do that?

In your prayer written below, ask God to help you:

Chapter · 28 ·

By Yourself, But Not Alone

Review Section III.
Read and reflect on these words in Deuteronomy 20:1:

> When you go to war against your enemies and see horses
> and chariots and an army greater than yours, do not be
> afraid of them, because the LORD your God, who brought
> you up out of Egypt, will be with you.

And Isaiah 43:2:

> "When you pass through the waters, I will be with you; and
> when you pass through the rivers, they will not sweep over
> you. When you walk through the fire, you will not be
> burned; the flames will not set you ablaze."

It's so hard to do some things alone—go to a new restaurant, new church, or a new job. It is much easier if I have a
friend or pal along. My good friend Judy and I do many
things together. We read the same books, search for many of
the same answers, and love going to the same church. We
have many of the same friends and much the same tastes.
But there are many things she can't do with me. As close as
we are, there are some things I have to face on my own.

I'd rather not have to deal with some situations, such as
working for someone whose vocabulary is peppered with ex-
pletives and cursing. It's very unpopular to take a stand for
righteousness and integrity when everyone around me is sug-

gesting compromise. It can be very lonely being left out of social circles because as a Christian I don't fit in. It's tough being the only one who doesn't laugh at dirty jokes or who thinks it's wrong to pilfer office supplies for personal use.

Sometimes you just have to make the decision to stand— all by yourself—to stick out, to be different. It's risky and, more often than not, without reward or affirmation.

There are those who can attest to being passed over for promotion because of their Christian standards, those who have lost sales because they wouldn't gloss over the truth. There are public servants who have lost favor because they wouldn't support gay or pro-abortion causes. Students who have lost grade points because of a strong Christian position in term papers, and teachers who have felt the sting of ungrateful remarks because they wouldn't look the other way when a student cheated.

Taking a stand can prove to be very unpopular. But if we don't, who will? If we can't, who can?

When you meet those times, remember this, you may be by yourself, but you're never alone. You have answered God's call to quiet. In your devotional life, you have taken the time to withdraw from the world and its influences, and now you can take the strength you gained there back into the everyday world where you live and work. You can actually return momentarily to being with God by taking an inward glance. Finding Him faithful with every breath you breathe. As close as your heartbeat, He is there.

I think it bears repeating: You may be by yourself, but you are never alone.

Consider these words of wisdom:

> It no longer matters to me what I may do, or what I may suffer, provided that I remain lovingly united to His will, which is my only concern.

> —Brother Lawrence, *Practicing the
> Presence of God*

Enjoy these words of beauty:

170

The Lord's our Rock, in Him we hide,
Secure whatever ill betide,
A shelter in the time of storm.

A shade by day, defense by night,
No fears alarm, no fears affright,
A shelter in the time of storm.

The raging storms may round us beat,
We'll never leave our safe retreat,
A shelter in the time of storm.

O Rock divine, O Refuge dear,
Be Thou our helper ever near,
A shelter in the time of storm.

Oh, Jesus is a Rock in a weary land,
A shelter in the time of storm.

—Vernon J. Charlesworth

Recall one experience when taking a firm stand personally cost you something you truly wanted.

When have you taken a stand for Christ and were disappointed by the reactions of those around you?

When have you ever taken a stand for Christ and felt that God disappointed you because of it?

How can you see this as a personal opportunity to grow?

In what ways can you be more secure when facing the world now that you have studied this lesson?

Write your prayer about this:

Chapter
· 29 ·

Keeping a
Quiet Heart

Review Section IV.
Read and reflect on these words from Proverbs 17:27:

A man of knowledge uses words with restraint. . . .

And Proverbs 21:23:

He who guards his mouth and his tongue keeps himself from calamity.

How many times have you left a meeting or gathering of friends and said, "I wish I would've kept my big mouth shut!" Or left work feeling as if you had blown your witness forever because of a careless remark or biting comment? Then, returning to God in quiet, you've repented your way back to peace. Isn't there some way to keep from putting our big feet squarely into our mouths at the most inopportune times?

After answering God's call to quiet, it isn't long before we experience a further call—a call to continue the quiet. To practice the quietness of God throughout our whole day.

Can you remember the last time you chose to hold your opinion to yourself, even when you were sure you were right? When you decisively restrained yourself from giving an idea in favor of letting someone else's idea be heard first? Taking God's quiet out of the devotional hour and into the busyness of life means that we learn to be quiet more and speak less.

173

I don't know about you, but it is so easy to catch myself mulling over my own thoughts, appearing to listen rather than really listening to someone else give their thoughts. I can even look like I'm intent upon their words, while I'm really only waiting until they stop, or take a breath, so I can jump in with carefully chosen comments of my own.

But when I let the quietness of God be more to me than just a few minutes during my devotional time, I find that in daily situations there is less need to always be the one speaking. It's so much easier to really listen to others when I'm quiet inside.

How do we tap into this quietness through days and routines that provide and encourage anything but quietness? Simply by turning our thoughts to Jesus once again.

Right there in the middle of a committee meeting, a parent-teacher conference, or choir practice, it's there—the quietness of God. Silently waiting to refresh me, noiselessly resting within my heart. It offers a stillness and calm affecting all of my life with a wisdom I do not possess on my own. It's amazing how we can listen to others, or pay attention to our daily tasks, yet allow for a connection between our inner selves and the quiet of God's presence within.

This is the secret: answering God's call to quiet—then taking that quiet with us.

A woman once asked, "When is it better to be silent?"

My response? *More often than I ever imagined.*

———————

Consider these words of wisdom:

> This is not a speculative devotion that can be practiced only in monasteries. Every one of us must adore God and love Him, and no one can discharge these two great duties without linking with them a heart relationship that makes us depend on Him every moment, like children who have difficulty standing up without their mother at their side.

> —Brother Lawrence, *Practicing the Presence of God*

Enjoy these words of beauty:

Jesus, the very thought of Thee
With sweetness fills my breast;
But sweeter far Thy face to see
And in Thy presence rest.

No voice can sing, no heart can frame,
Nor can the memory find
A sweeter sound than Thy blest name,
O Savior of mankind!

O hope of every contrite heart,
O joy of all the meek,
To those who fall, how kind Thou art!
How good to those who seek!

But what to those who find? Ah, this
No tongue nor pen can show,
The love of Jesus, what it is,
None but His loved ones know.

—Translated from the Latin by
Edward Caswall

Looking over the past week, how can you see that keeping
a quiet heart might have helped you in a particular situation?
Comment:

When was it hard to keep your mouth shut and maintain a
quietness?

In all honesty, within the past week or two, how many times
can you recall giving unsolicited advice that began with such
words as "You need to . . ."?

How many times have you had an answer ready before a question was fully asked?

Ecclesiastes, chapter three, says, "There is . . . a time to be silent and a time to speak." How can you make sure you determine those times accurately?

Write any further thoughts or prayers here:

Chapter · 30 ·

Stand Back and Wait

Review Section V.
Read Psalm 27 and reflect on these words from verse 14:

> *Wait for the* LORD; *be strong and take heart and wait for the* LORD.

Once we have learned to wait quietly before the Lord in our quiet times, finally tuning in not only to His word but to His presence, it isn't long before a situation arises that provides an opportunity to wait *for the Lord* outside the quietness of our devotional time. Painful or awkward circumstances often tempt us to rush in with words or actions meant to "fix" a situation. The last thing that seems appropriate to do is *nothing*. Yet, though that appears to be the case, sometimes it is the exact approach to take. But we're not talking about the avoidance kind of nothing, or the "ignore it" kind of nothing. It isn't denial, either. It's the nothing that is *waiting*.

This kind of do-nothing approach isn't a passive, evasive nonaction. It is a wait-and-see-what-the-Lord-will-do, submissive approach—not to the situation, but to God.

When you answer God's call to quiet, He may show you when this quietness means you are to take a "stand back" position to circumstances and problems in your daily life. Stand back? Shirk responsibility? By no means! Take the responsibility to seek God *first*, before you react. Retouch that quietness and allow it to affect life's difficult decisions. Let a quiet pause answer your accuser while you stand by for God's direction.

To take such action, we have to decide to be patient and trust God. To purposely put whatever comes at us in His hands. To let Him work at both ends of the situation at the same time. To give Him control. To do that means we decide to *not* trust ourselves, to *not* take matters into our own hands, to *not* work it out in our own strength. It means we give up control.

That's only possible when we have determined to give our life, warts and all, to God. When we ask God to help us out of some mess we've created, we stand back and watch Him work, even if it's uncomfortable for us to stay out of it.

When we answer God's call to quiet, we're not only agreeing that we need more quiet time, that life has become much too noisy and busy and we need the therapeutic effects of silence and solitude. Rather, we are submitting to God at a level deeper than ever before. We are seeking Him before we seek His gifts, blessings, or wisdom. We are accepting His call to quietness in all of life. The quiet time is only the beginning.

As you come to the end of this study, have the courage to take the things learned here into all of your life. Let these principles calm your pressured existence, bring order to your chaotic life, and let the God of hope fill you with all joy and peace. (See Romans 15:13.)

Consider these words of wisdom:

> This sums up our entire call of duty: to adore God and to love Him, without worrying about the rest.
>
> —Brother Lawrence, *Practicing the Presence of God*

Enjoy these words of beauty:

> Blessed assurance, Jesus is mine!
> Oh, what a foretaste of glory divine!
> Heir of salvation, purchase of God,

Born of His spirit, washed in His blood.

Perfect submission, perfect delight,
Visions of rapture now burst on my sight;
Angels descending bring from above
Echoes of mercy, whispers of love.

Perfect submission, all is at rest,
I in my Savior am happy and blest;
Watching and waiting, looking above,
Filled with His goodness, lost in His love.

This is my story, this is my song:
Praising my Savior all the day long;
This is my story, this is my song:
Praising my Savior all the day long.

—Fanny J. Crosby

———

How has the pace of your life changed since you began this study?

How has your inner pace changed?

What areas of rush and busyness do you still struggle with?

179

How can you apply the things learned here to those areas?

What changes do you see in your relationship with God?

How will you keep those changes going and growing to influence your life even more?

Write a summary of what you have learned in this study in a prayer to God:

Leader's Notes

GROUP GUIDELINE SUGGESTIONS

If this study is used in a group setting, it's important for the group's purpose to be clearly stated. Ask yourself first, then the group, "Why does this group exist, and what do we hope to accomplish by being together for the time it will take to study this book?" By clearly defining your purpose, the group process will be more beneficial for everyone committed to the study.

At the first meeting, go over the group's purpose, or reason for being (in more formal settings this could be written out as a mission statement), and read together the preface to the book. Discuss the busyness of contemporary life, how it robs us of peace, and the need for times of quietness and a closer relationship with God. Pray together at the end of the discussion that God's purposes will be accomplished in each individual's life, that His presence will be felt at the meetings, and that all will have open hearts to listen and learn what He wants to teach through this study.

Throughout each week, members are to study individually each of the five entries in the next section of the book. This prepares them for discussion at the next weekly meeting. A group may decide to spend more or less time on a given section, according to the needs or wishes of the group. You may choose to discuss any of the response questions at the end of each lesson or study. Additional questions are in these leader's notes.

A good general group approach to this study is one of personal investigation and shared responses. Discussion questions will help bring out even more insight into application for personal growth.

In the course of covering the material, some very private areas of personal discovery may be exposed or brought to mind. Leaders should be sensitive and not expect, or force, everyone to participate each time or respond to each discussion question. Do encourage even the slightest participation with affirmative comments, regardless of the contribution.

Because this is a responsive study, there are no wrong answers. The nature of the study tends to get to the heart of many emotional issues. Some people in your group may desperately need a listening ear, and a correction from you may discourage them from participating in the discussion, or even from attending your group again. Allow the Holy Spirit to do the correcting in others and a deep work of patience and sensitivity in you, the leader.

Once in a while, there will be a member of a group who monopolizes the conversation or goes off on a tangent. If this happens, very carefully approach that person afterward and ask if you can be of help individually. There may be times during the study when a person may genuinely come to a breakthrough, drawing the attention of the group to herself and her needs exclusively. That would be the exception, however, and not the rule.

If someone in your group asks a question, don't take the sole responsibility for having an answer. Allow others in the group to contribute. If you do give an answer, try waiting until after the others have spoken.

There are three basic rules that promote healthy group

meetings and encourage close openness between your members:

1. *Start and end on schedule.* Everyone is busy, and starting and ending on time shows respect and understanding for the pressures in each of our lives. One and a half hours generally works well for evening groups. Daytime groups may want to meet for a little longer. Sunday school groups, of course, meet within an assigned schedule. Actual study and discussion should take only a portion of the meeting time. Fellowship and sharing prayer requests help develop strong bonds within your group. Don't be afraid to make time for that to happen.

2. *Begin and end with prayer.* The opening prayer can be a simple offering by one person asking God's blessing on your time together. You may feel the need in your group to have additional time for prayer concerns or needs of the group. One effective way to handle this is to have everyone write down the name of the person they are concerned for and a very brief statement about the need on a small piece of paper. The slips are put into a basket and redistributed to the group. Each person then offers a short prayer concerning the request they have drawn from the basket, then makes a commitment to pray for the need during the week between the meetings. Closing prayers should be centered around the needs that have arisen related to the study and discussion. Bring the meeting to a close with your own prayer.

3. *Involve everyone.* Many of the issues covered in this study are of a deep, personal nature. Depending on the amount of abuse or misunderstanding your group members have experienced, some may not be ready to discuss the issues they are dealing with. However, during the fellowship time, the time of praying for others, and the ongoing study, seek to create a trustworthy place that will encourage them to be open with the group as much as possible. Find ways to involve even the most reserved people, making them feel comfortable and safe.

Discussion times can be rich and rewarding for everyone—that is, everyone who gets to share and discuss. The size of the group somewhat determines the opportunities for sharing. A group of six members is ideal, but a group as large as ten can work. When the group reaches ten, consider the advantages of dividing into smaller groups of three or four for at least a portion of the sharing and discussion time.

Discussion Questions

Orientation—Introduction
   It is helpful to have an orientation meeting before you begin a group study of this book. Such a meeting will allow members of the group to have an opportunity to look over the book and to prepare for the first discussion and sharing time.
   The following questions will help your group members get off to a good start and understand what to expect during the study.

1. Many people have difficulty fitting a daily quiet time into their busy routine. In what ways have you tried to do this? What has worked for you, and what hasn't?
2. Read aloud the preface to the book, then ask: How has the noise of our contemporary society robbed us of silence? Solitude?
3. How do you think the busyness of modern life affects our relationship with God?
4. When we read a book or embark on a new study, not every illustration or example fits our own particular situation. Yet we might find such an illustration to be helpful in some way. Why do you think this could be true?
5. Read aloud the introduction to the first section, then ask: When you hear that God wants to invite you to come away with Him, what is the first thing that enters your mind?
6. Could you use some unrushed time in God's presence? What would you expect to get out of it? If possible, share those thoughts in prayer form. Pray together.

Assignment
   Everyone should first read "How to Use This Book" at the beginning of the book. Each day for five days before the

184

next meeting, read and respond to each of the devotional studies in Section I, "Come Away...". (This will be the weekly routine for personal preparation for each meeting.)

Section I: Come Away . . .

Begin this meeting time by reading again the introduction to the section. Then use the following questions as models or thought-starters for group discussion:

1. In our busy lives, are we more apt to view a daily quiet time as discipline or desired time with the Lord?
2. Have you been taught to take time away from pressing responsibilities to spend with Him alone? Comment.
3. In the introduction, the image of a little girl bowing low in the presence of a king is presented. How does that illustration help or hinder you in answering God's call to quiet?
4. What distractions did you have to handle to "come away" with God this week?
5. What was your favorite lesson? Why?
6. How can we pray to help each of you answer God's call to quiet this week? Pray together.

Section II: Come Alone

Read together the introduction to the section and then discuss the following:

1. Do you embrace or avoid the concept of solitude?
2. Is it scary to be in God's presence alone? Why or why not?
3. What things, issues, or people put pressure on your efforts to be alone with God?
4. What other distractions did you have to handle to be alone with God this week?
5. What was your favorite lesson? Why?
6. What lesson or question gave you difficulty? Why?
7. What prayers do you need from the group to help you come *away, alone* this week? Pray together.

Section III: Come Quietly

Read together the introduction to the section and then discuss the following:

185

1. What would it mean to you if you knew you had God's undivided attention?
2. What noises fill your home? Which would you like to silence if you could?
3. What's it like to spend five minutes in total silence? To find out, set a timer, then ask the group to spend three to five minutes in silence. Discuss their reactions.
4. Why do you think we fight or resist silence?
5. What was your favorite lesson, quote, or poem from this part of the book? Why?
6. Which lesson didn't you like or made you uncomfortable? Why?
7. Share prayer requests for next week and pray together.

Sections III to V
(Follow this format until you reach Section VI.)
Read aloud the introduction to the section in the book studied individually since the last meeting.

1. By this time the group should be more willing to share without much prodding from you. Asking more simple, general questions will lead your group to share more of themselves, not simply discuss the material. Questions like:
   A. How are you doing with the study so far?
   B. What changes are you seeing in your quiet times?
   C. What difficulties are you having?
   D. What quote was your favorite this week? Why?
   E. How can this group help you?
2. Pray together.
3. At the end of Section V, you might want to discuss what your group would like to study next.

Section VI: Taking the Quiet With You
Read the introduction to this final section together and discuss the following:

1. How have you tried to take the presence of God from your quiet time into the mainstream of your life? With what result?
2. Can any of you share a recent experience where you were

faced with a situation and you knew you had to purposely "stay away" from it?
3. How have you experienced God's presence with you this week?
4. How is it easier to "go it alone" now than when you began this study? (Refer to Chapter 28.)
5. Can you name a time you chose to remain quiet this week? And with what result?
6. How have you experienced releasing control? What happened? (Refer to Chapter 30.)
7. How has this study been of benefit to you? How has your relationship with God changed because of it?
8. Pray together.
9. Where do we go from here? (As a group, individuals, next study, etc.)

Bibliography

Brother Lawrence. *Practicing the Presence of God*. Paraclete Press.

Fenelon. *Let Go*. Springdale, Pa.: Whitaker House.

Foster, Richard J. *Celebration of Discipline*. San Francisco: HarperSan Francisco.

———. *Prayer, Finding the Heart's True Home*. HarperCollins

Frye, Stephen D. *Quiet Times Dynamics*, Pathfinder Pamphlets. Downer's Grove, Ill.: InterVarsity Press.

Hazard, David, ed. *Mighty Is Your Hand*. Minneapolis: Bethany House.

———. *You Give Me New Life* by the Early Disciples. Minneapolis: Bethany House.

MacDonald, Gordon. *Restoring Your Spiritual Passion*. Nashville: Thomas Nelson, Inc.

Merton, Thomas. *Contemplative Prayer*. Image Publishers.

M'Intyre, David. *Hidden Life of Prayer*. Minneapolis: Bethany House.

Murray, Andrew. *Waiting on God*. Chicago: Moody Press.

Runcorn, David. *A Center of Quiet*. Downers Grove, Ill.: InterVarsity Press.

Tozer, A. W. *The Pursuit of God*, Christian Publications, Inc.